THE
ORDINATION
OF WOMEN

*Fourteenth Century Fresco Depicting Holy Spirit as a Female
Between the Father on the Left and the Son on the Right,
Urschalling Church, Bavaria.
Original photo by Wolfgang Schreiner, Germany.*

THE ORDINATION OF WOMEN

An Essay on the Office of
Christian Ministry

by

Paul K. Jewett

Professor of Systematic Theology
Fuller Theological Seminary

WILLIAM B. EERDMANS PUBLISHING COMPANY
GRAND RAPIDS, MICHIGAN

To the Women Who Have Been My Students
—and My Teachers

Copyright © 1980 by Wm. B. Eerdmans Publishing Co.
255 Jefferson Ave. S.E., Grand Rapids, Mich. 49503

Library of Congress Cataloging in Publication Data

Jewett, Paul King.
  The ordination of women.

  1. Ordination of women.   I. Title
BV676.J48   262'.14   80-15644
ISBN 0-8028-1850-1

Contents

Preface

The dedication of this book provides a clue to the reason that the author wrote it and how he comes to his conclusions about the ordination of women: he listens to what women are saying about themselves! Since I have been a teacher myself, I know the truth of learning from one's students. But I sense a wider meaning in Paul Jewett's words, a meaning which is a key to the forward movement of the liberation of all persons. Dr. Jewett is willing to place himself in the stance of a student capable of learning from, rather than defining (and thereby limiting), those with whom he is in dialogue—in this case, women. Liberated persons "name" themselves, instead of living within the confines of others' notions of their identity or what they are capable of accomplishing. It is within this larger context of feminine subordination/liberation that the question of the ordination of women arises.

There is only one point in this book where I find myself questioning Dr. Jewett's exposition. His presentation of ministry in the Roman Catholic Church limits it to the clergy. Ministry is a broader concept within our tradition than appears here. We, too, assert that all Christians minister, but in a variety of ways. Ministry is not a sacrament; Holy Orders is a sacrament which enables a man (to date) to minister differently from the way Sisters, Brothers, and other lay Catholics minister in our world. However, this difference in the interpretation of the Catholic and Protestant positions in no way detracts from the lucid treatment of each of the arguments against women's ordination in this book.

I was particularly struck by the emphasis on the fluctuation between the literal and symbolic interpretations of the reasons against the ordination of women in Chapter Four. We do, indeed, need to develop ("convert") our imaginations, as Dr. Jewett demonstrates. A second matter of significance to me is the author's stress on the fact that God is beyond sexuality, and therefore our concept of the divine cannot be limited to masculine biblical imagery; feminine as well as neuter symbols for God surface in the Bible and enhance our understanding greatly if we attend to them.

I am delighted that Dr. Paul Jewett continues to research and publish these works, thereby contributing his name to the growing number of men and women who combat discrimination *within* the very Church that preaches "all are one in Christ."

JOAN HENEHAN, C.S.J.
Member, Women's Ordination Conference

Los Angeles, California
May 1980

Abstract of the Argument

Postulating a partnership of the sexes as the Christian ideal for all of life, I seek in the following study to show how this ideal may be more adequately achieved in the church of Christ. My thesis is that the woman, as the man's equal, should share with him in all aspects of the church's life and mission. Specifically, this means that she should have full access to the privileges and responsibilities of the Christian ministry. I review the traditional grounds for excluding women from ordination to this office, beginning with the argument from the nature of woman, proceeding to that of the nature of the ministerial office, and concluding with that of the nature of God himself. This last argument—wherein it is assumed that the masculinity of God entails a male order of ministry—occupies the largest place in the discussion. This is due to the many issues which such an argument raises, such as the meaning of biblical language about God, the nature of the Incarnation, and the implications of an exclusively male apostolate. This section concludes with an analysis and appraisal of the Vatican Declaration, "Inter Insigniores," against the ordination of women to the ministerial priesthood.

Having reviewed these several arguments, and having rejected them as resting on an inadequate understanding of biblical revelation, I then raise the question of what should be done in order that the Christian woman may enter into her full inheritance in the church as a minister of Jesus Christ. The suggestions I make bear particularly on matters of graduate education as it has traditionally been offered in the theological seminary. I make the plea that qualified women who are open to God's call to the ministry be recruited and trained as men have been in the past. My thought is not that they should be trained to fulfill their calling as though they were men, but rather that they should be so trained as to qualify for the tasks of responsible leadership in the church hithertofore reserved for men. I do not attempt to give answers to all the many practical questions such a position raises. My concern is rather that Christian women shall have the freedom, which is their right as persons, to hear and answer the call of God as in the past men have heard and answered it; in other words, that they shall have the freedom to know the full meaning of what Martin Luther called *The Liberty of the Christian*.[1]

I do not, in this essay, deal in any detailed way with the Pauline injunction to silence imposed upon women in church nor with the limitation placed upon their teaching in the Pastoral Epistles, since these matters are part of the larger question of the hierarchy of the sexes, a question which I discuss elsewhere.[2] I do, however, in several addenda of varying length, touch on certain matters related to the discussion: the difference between the priestly and the prophetic offices; the effort to understand the Holy Spirit as female; the question of deaconesses in the New Testament; and the meaning of motherhood. In the final section (Epilogue) I explore the problem of sexist language, focusing especially on the question of how such language may be changed in the hymnal and the Bible. The suggestions made (often tentative in nature) and the conclusions reached are an effort to advance the problem a little way

---

[1]*Von der Freiheit eines Christenmenschen* is literally translated, "Concerning the Liberty of a Christian Man." We are here abbreviating Luther's title in order to enlarge the scope of his thesis—a little exercise in Christian liberty.
[2]See my *Man as Male and Female* (Grand Rapids: Eerdmans, 1975).

toward a solution. Since the problem is deeper than language, the solution must go beyond a change of language. In the interest of contributing to such a larger change, I challenge, in the following pages, the traditional view that the ministerial office belongs exclusively to men and argue for the woman's right to exercise the priesthood of all believers as it is individually expressed in that office.

May I, in conclusion, express my gratitude to the women who have sat in my lectures and interacted with my thought. I am especially indebted to Dr. Marguerite Shuster, who made numerous editorial suggestions of a most helpful nature, as to both the literary form of the argument and its material content.

Pasadena
December, 1979

I
Introduction

Throughout the centuries of church history there has been little serious discussion of woman's ordination to the office of Christian ministry; the debate is a contemporary one.[1] In this particular study our purpose is to illumine the discussion not so much from the perspective of practical considerations as from that of theological principle. Those who would deny women access to the ministry have, in the last analysis, done so on principle; they have argued that there are some deep and significant reasons in the very nature of things why men and only men should be ministers in Christ's church. Though stated somewhat differently by those in the Roman and Anglo-Catholic communions than by those in Protestant communions, these reasons are not limited to any theological tradition; they have, rather, an ecumenical scope.[2] Since the argument from "the nature of things," when spelled out, includes the nature of woman, the nature of the ministerial office, and the nature of God himself, we shall follow this order in the ensuing argument.

---

[1]In this study we shall simply assume that Christian ministry in the church involves an "office," though the term, as such, does not occur in the New Testament. The important matter, as we see it, is not the use of the term as such but the qualification of the term as the office of *Christian ministry.*

[2]We will, however, give attention to certain specific and unique aspects of Eastern Orthodox and Roman Catholic teaching on the sacramental order of ministry in due time. See below, especially "Concerning the Vatican Decree 'Inter Insigniores,'" pp. 74–97.

Thus we shall move from the periphery to the heart of the issue.

As we turn to the discussion of these matters, it remains to be observed that we view the question of women in the ministry as an instance of the larger issue: How ought men and women to be related in life generally? Because this latter question is so fundamental, involving as it does the very meaning of human existence as male and female, we can do little more than state our position at this point and refer the reader for its elaboration and defense to another place.[3]

The position we espouse as biblical is one which views the relationship of the man to the woman as a partnership in life, especially in the life of the Christian church. Partnership, we believe, is the implication both of the creation ordinance whereby God made humankind in his image as male and female (Gen. 1:26), and of the new creation in Christ, in which the barriers of race (Jew and Greek), class (bond and free), and sex (male and female) are done away with (Gal. 3:26–28).[4] For this reason we reject the traditional view of sexual hierarchy, according to which the man, as such, is the head of the woman, and the woman, as such, is subordinate to the man. We subscribe rather to the view that under God men and women, as partners in life, share its privileges and responsibilities together. Of course, since men and women are different, sharing the privileges and responsibilities of life in the church does not mean that women should now do everything that men have done in the past any more than that men should continue, in an exclusive way, to do many things that women might also do. Partnership means complementarity, not competitiveness. What such sharing may mean concretely, we can say only as

[3]See my *Man as Male and Female* (Grand Rapids: Eerdmans, 1975). This study, which constitutes a kind of theological prolegomenon to all specific questions of male/female relationships, including the relationship of clergy and laity in the church, is undertaken in the larger context of the ongoing theological discussion concerning the nature of humankind as in the divine image.

[4]To speak of Jew and Greek in terms of "race" is admittedly not altogether accurate, but the point we are making remains unaffected.

we learn through the experience of relationship itself what God's will, in this regard, for his church may be.

Actually, because of the stultifying effects of male domination in the past, we are just beginning in our society to discover the resources of the woman. And this is true even in the church, though, indeed, through the centuries women have been given sufficient responsibility as members of Christ's body to remove all reasonable doubt about their potential for leadership in the worship of God and witness to his word. In saying as much, we have in mind more than their traditional contribution in the servant role of deaconess and in the maternal roles of Sunday school teacher and minister of Christian education. On the mission field women have proved their ability to function in many ways proscribed to their sex at home; and, if we can believe the testimony of history, in medieval Europe ordained abbesses were sometimes given the same authority as men. Not only did they have the right to hear confession, to preach, and to read the Scripture in public; they also administered ecclesiastical and religious estates, presided over religious ceremonies involving both men and women, and were invested with cope, miter, and stole.[5]

But, as we said, our task and concern is, first of all, not practical but theological in nature; we must analyze those matters of principle which bear on the question of women in the ministry. Since correct theological principle, which is biblically informed and derived, is the basis of good order in Christ's church, we must begin with an analysis which reflects this priority. In this analysis, as we noted, we shall consider first the nature of woman, move on to that of the ministerial office, and conclude with some reflections on the nature of God himself.

[5]See Joan Morris, *The Lady Was a Bishop* (New York: The Macmillan Co., 1973), a study which seeks to document the thesis that what Rome now officially forswears to women was for centuries allowed, at least in some instances.

II.
The Argument from the Nature of Woman That Women Should Not Be Admitted to the Order of Ministry in the Church

A. A STATEMENT OF THE ARGUMENT

As we have observed, serious debate over woman's right to the holy office of Christian ministry is a comparatively modern phenomenon. Throughout Christian history it has been more or less taken for granted that women should not be admitted to the ranks of the ordained clergy for the obvious reason that they are women. By the same token, when theologians have paused to discuss the matter briefly, their remarks have often reflected their view of women more than their view of the ministry, though of course the two are related, as the title of this study implies.

To the question, "What is woman?" The early Fathers of the church answered that she is "the devil's gateway," though one woman in due time was recognized as "the Queen of Heaven." One cannot but pause in astonishment over such a paradox. How could the same creature be loaded with such opprobrium and yet exalted to such honor? Whatever hidden explanations for this ambivalence may lurk in the depth of the male psyche, the biblical reasons which the early teachers of the church gave for their repudiation-in-affirmation of the woman are clear enough, if not convincing. As the apostle Paul in Romans 5 compared Adam with Christ, so they compared Eve with Mary. As "with rash hand in evil hour," Eve plucked the fruit that was the ruin of us all, so Mary, the handmaid of the Lord, by her *fiat mihi* of humble submission (Luke 1:38), brought salvation to us all.

But it is doubtful that this homage paid the second Eve compensated for the wrong done the first Eve. In the latter instance the church Fathers were really emulating the example of fallen Adam, who blamed the woman rather than confess his own guilt when confronted with the searching question: "Have you eaten of the tree?" (Gen. 3:11–12). Blinded by the prejudice which led them to fault the woman as the first to offend God's law, it seems never to have occurred to the Fathers that the specific shortcomings of the feminine sex, with which they were familiar, might be due not to an essential weakness of character but to the disabilities inflicted by Greco-Roman culture. For them the woman, *per definitionem*, was the "weaker vessel," "slow of understanding," "unstable in mind," "liable to deception," the one whose disobedience had ruined the man, the image and glory of God, and required the death of the Son of God.[1]

Many of the ancient Fathers were aided and abetted in this deep suspicion of the female by their view of human sexuality. Reacting to the pervasive license of their day and, in some instances, lamenting the power of lust in their own lives before conversion, they embraced a rigorous asceticism

---

[1]"The second [reason why Paul instructs Timothy not to grant authority in the church to women] shows how female leadership led to disaster in Paradise, and a possible repetition of that must be avoided. The great catastrophe took place under female guidance; the events of the fall of man are like a beacon, warning voyagers of the future to stay clear of that channel" (see the letter by L. Mulder in *The Reformed Journal*, September 1979, p. 10). Note the date. Some arguments die hard!

which inevitably distorted their perception. They not only uncritically assumed the androcentricity of their culture, whereby in all things men are ordained to rule and women to obey, but often went beyond this to portray the woman as a subtle and dangerous creature "whose heart is snares and nets" and "whose hands are as bands" from which the unwary shall not escape (Eccles. 7:26). Woman, in the vulgar eloquence of Chrysostom, was "a necessary evil, a natural temptation, a desirable calamity, a domestic peril, a painted ill."[2]

While the leading schoolmen of the Middle Ages did not indulge such emotional displays of prejudice, they too assumed, without debate, the superiority of the man over the woman as the one in whom "the discretion of reason predominates" (Thomas Aquinas). Even in procreation, the one and only work in which she is man's indispensible collaborator, the woman was seen as a mere recipient whose role is one of passive submission.

Although the period of the late Middle Ages was distinguished by an emphasis on the concept of romantic love, it was also marred by a superstitious obsession with witchcraft, a mania from which even the Protestant Reformers did not escape.[3] For many, witches, with their broomsticks and sabbaths, have long since been remanded to oblivion, but the demeaning legacy of the past is not easily exorcised from the church's view of women. While the image of woman as the "devil's gateway" has undoubtedly relinquished much

---

[2]As quoted by Kathleen Bliss, *The Service and Status of Women in the Churches* (London: S.C.M. Press, 1952). For other specific sources in patristic literature—Tertullian, Ambrose, Jerome *et al.*—see D. S. Bailey, *Sexual Relations in Christian Thought* (New York: Harper & Bros., 1959), p. 63. This attitude helps one understand why celibacy was made the ideal for the clergy long before it was implemented in reality. Marriage came to be regarded as a concession to human frailty incompatible with the fullest devotion to the service of God.

[3]The authors of the medieval handbook on witchcraft, *Malleus Maleficarum (The Witches' Hammer)*, inform their readers that the title of their book is in the feminine since the overwhelming majority of those who have commerce with demons are women. Because the woman is frivolous, given to obscene curiosity and duplicity, there are many witches; by contrast, there are few wizards because of the natural vigor of the male mind to resist temptation!

of its traditional power over the minds of men, in the contemporary debate about her qualifications for the Christian ministry the woman is still accused of being the vehicle of temptation in the male.

In his discussion of women in the priesthood, E. L. Mascall, prominent theological spokesman for high-church Anglicanism, refers to N. P. Williams' "imposing argument" against their ordination. Williams (as quoted by Mascall) bases his argument on the "well-known, though mysterious, affinity between religious emotion and sex-emotion" in virtue of which "the stimulation of the religious instinct may, by a kind of subconscious reverberation, under certain circumstances, simultaneously stimulate that *per se* less supernatural instinct which is so closely allied to it." Therefore it becomes a matter of

> the utmost importance, indeed ... the most stringent necessity, that the personality of the officient in any form of divine worship, as of any others who in any degree participate in the leadership of worship ... should not be such as to convey, even accidentally, the very slightest avoidable suggestion, of the kind which we have indicated, to the imaginations of any present.[4]

The natural conclusion to such an argument is that only those ought to be admitted to holy orders whose personal presence is not likely, in a liturgical or sacramental atmosphere, to exercise any distracting effect upon worshipers of the opposite sex. Williams, as quoted by Mascall, claims that

> men as such are very less likely to be an involuntary cause of distraction to women, under the circumstances of public worship, than women are to men; and that this is a permanent fact of human nature,

---

[4]E. L. Mascall, "Women and the Priesthood of the Church," *Why Not? Priesthood and the Ministry of Women*, ed. Michael Bruce and G. E. Duffield (Appleford: Marcham Manor Press, 1972), p. 99, quoting from an address of N. P. Williams, delivered at the Convocation of Canterbury, June 1938.

> which can no more be abolished by modern progress than the law of gravitation can be abolished by modern progress.[5]

He hastens to add that

> although this fact may seem to result in a privilege for men, it does not imply any moral superiority on their part over women, but, if anything, the opposite; it is based, paradoxically enough, upon their greater weakness (in this regard) and susceptibility.[6]

Anglicans are not alone in such reasoning. In a more recent statement, the Rev. Herbert Carson, an English Baptist minister, deplores a false delicacy in discussing the matter of women ministering to men, a delicacy which he feels is contrary to biblical realism. The New Testament warns against the lustful look, he reminds us, and admonishes women to modesty in dress, and that not without reason. Put bluntly, he says, the issue is simply this:

> If a man stands in a pulpit the average woman is not unduly affected by his appearance: but if a woman stands there, men, being men, will often find that their thoughts are less on the word spoken than on the speaker. Someone will reply indignantly that "to the pure all things are pure." But we are forced to admit that not all men are pure, and, in fact, for the majority of men the battle with impure thoughts is a lot more severe than the average woman realizes. The pulpit which is to be a help towards holiness should not provide an additional snare—which of course it will not do if its normal occupant is a man.[7]

---

[5]Mascall, *ibid.* The senate of the state of Florida voted down the Equal Rights Amendment after senator Lew Brantley warned, "The effect on society would be like repealing the law of gravity" (see the *Los Angeles Times*, April 26, 1974). To liken the attraction of the sexes for each other to the law of gravity, which describes the attraction of physical bodies for each other, is plausible enough. But for males to argue that this attraction works only one way when it comes to the female privilege of ministry hardly commends the males' vaunted powers of superior reasoning!

[6]Mascall, *ibid.*

[7]*Reformation Today*, no. 5 (Spring, 1971), p. 9.

B. A RESPONSE TO THE ARGUMENT

Such an argument, if it proves anything, proves too much. As Mascall admits, pressed to its logical conclusion it would exclude women from any visible, official participation in worship; and, unless the senses of sight and sound are fundamentally different, it would appear also to exclude them from participating in an invisible choir, a restriction beyond the limitations imposed even by the Eastern Orthodox and Roman Catholic communions.[8]

Furthermore, to limit the argument to a strictly religious context and allow that, although she may not lead the worshiping congregation, a woman may deliver lectures to a mixed class in a university, only reminds one acquainted with history that it was not always so. Novella d'Andrea (A.D. 1312–66), one of the few women admitted to a chair in the venerable University of Bologna, lectured on philosophy and law behind a curtain, lest her face distract her male students. If men students have learned to concentrate on lectures by a woman without the aid of a curtain, why may men parishioners not achieve a similar discipline in a worship service when all due proprieties are observed? The answer has been given that in a purely secular context the situation is not surcharged with the same emotion as in a service of worship. But in those very communions where such a distinction is most commonly made, women have functioned as readers and as godmothers at baptisms; and, according to Roman Catholic theory, in a wedding Mass the bride is the minister of a public sacrament.[9]

In truth, the argument against women ministers taken from "male weakness," disarming as it may seem, is just about as bankrupt as an argument can be. It is but a

---

[8]In the West, in the seventeenth and eighteenth centuries, the church used "artificial" male sopranos and contraltos, the so-called *castrati*. But this custom was only indirectly related to the question at hand.

[9]See Mascall, "Women and the Priesthood of the Church," pp. 101–11, where he admits that in the light of such considerations it is difficult to build an argument on *psychological* considerations for the incapacity of women to receive holy orders, or, for that matter, even the impropriety that they should.

thinly veiled admission that the woman is still regarded as a sex object rather than as a person. And if this is so, rather than limiting the woman in her freedom as a child of God, men ought to redeem the man/woman relationship in the church by repenting of their sins.[10]

In all fairness, it must be said that probably the great majority have done so and that the sexual problem, at the physical level, is of little consequence today. But what many men, including clergymen, do not realize is that even when their relationship to women has been redeemed to a degree more worthy of Christian fellowship in the body of Christ, they still regard women as different from themselves in that, as men, they are *capable* of erotic love, while women are *made* for it. Not that they would be so crass as Nietzsche— "when a woman inclines to learning there is usually something wrong with her sex apparatus"—but they still have not transcended the traditional stereotype. A Paul may remain unmarried throughout life for the gospel's sake, and this is praiseworthy; a Luther may delay marriage for the same reason, and this is praiseworthy too; but a woman is made for marriage; her chief end is to glorify God—as a wife.[11] As Byron wrote:

> Man's love is of man's life a thing apart:
> 'Tis woman's whole existence.

[10]We might at this point observe that a redeemed man/woman relationship will adorn the woman in the pulpit as a person (perhaps with a robe), and this should be of some help. The Hollywood star whose long nails deprive her hands of their usefulness, the office girl who is paralyzed by her clothes and petrified by her makeup because she is a body and exists for the desire it arouses, will never invade the pulpit if she is not placed there by men. The 1500 prostitutes (*Dirnen* is the word used by W. D. Marsch, *RGG*, "Frau," III, B, "In der Kirchengeschichte," b.s. 1072) reportedly present at the Council of Constance were hardly all permanent residents of the town!

[11]The prestigious eleventh edition of the *Encyclopedia Britannica* endorses the theory that Elizabeth, queen of England, never married because "debarred from matrimony by a physical defect," citing no other basis for this judgment than "contemporary gossip which was probably justified." However, in some recent biographical studies a good case has been made for the thesis that she avoided marriage for the simple reason that she perceived that all her suitors had designs on her throne.

It is this very attitude on the part of men that has made it so difficult for women to transcend the erotic, even in a religious situation. That women should prove a "distraction" to men in a context of public worship is not at all "a permanent fact of human nature," like the law of gravity. It is rather the result of the man's having shut the woman up to erotic love as her only proper vocation.[12]

It is basically this same attitude that leads men to joke about women preachers or cringe at the prospect of relating to them in a pastoral role. Johnson's celebrated remark when Boswell told him that he had gone on a Sunday morning to a Quaker meeting and heard a woman preach, reflects the assumption that a woman who preaches has left her proper province: "Sir, a woman's preaching is like a dog walking on its hinder legs. It is not done well; but you are surprised to find it done at all."[13]

Such humor did not pass away in the eighteenth century. Reflecting aversion to the thought of confessing to women priests, a contemporary German author, Ida Friederika Gorres, comments, "What a kaleidoscope of situations we should have, embarrassing, grotesque, delicate, amusing and quite intolerable." On this matter Mary Daly

[12]*Variety Magazine* called Aimee Semple McPherson, preacher of the Foursquare Gospel, "sexy but Episcopalian, an angel with an oblique Mona Lisa smile." When she preached in England, the *London Daily Mail* commented on her short skirts, flesh-colored stockings, and elaborate coiffure, sometimes Titian-red, sometimes blond, always her own. Asked by reporters years after her "kidnapping" if she intended to marry again, she replied, "My life will always be for Jesus" (see Ishbeh Ross, *Charmers and Cranks* [New York: Harper & Row, 1965], pp. 252ff.). This last remark about living only "for Jesus" reminds one of the eroticism found in female religious mystics throughout the ages. Catherine of Siena (A.D. 1347–80), perhaps the greatest of them all, claimed to have been given a wedding ring by Jesus which was the ring of flesh cut off at his circumcision. In St. Theresa's famous vision, where a golden dart is plunged into her heart, she testifies, "I am certain that the pain penetrated my deepest entrails and it seemed as if they were torn when my spiritual spouse withdrew the arrow with which he had penetrated them" (as cited in Simone de Beauvoir, *The Second Sex* [New York: Alfred A. Knopf, Inc., 1968], pp. 632–33).

[13]George B. Hill, ed., *Boswell's Life of Johnson* (New York: Harper & Bros., 1891), 1:535.

retorts that the centuries in which women have been compelled to make confession to men furnish not only *imagined* but *real* situations that are indeed embarrassing, grotesque, delicate, amusing, and quite intolerable.[14] Even more scathing is the observation of Simone de Beauvoir that men have always written the rules which—if we are to believe the theologians—God has ordained. According to these rules, man holds the powerful weapons of ablution and excommunication; thus, the church sees to it that God never authorizes the woman to escape male guardianship.[15]

---

[14] *The Church and the Second Sex* (New York: Harper & Row, 1968), p. 154.

[15] *The Second Sex*, pp. 585–88. One whose consciousness is awakened will eschew not only the crude humor that has marked the male as a chauvinist, but also the unwitting yet demeaning allusions to women, so familiar to us all. Consider, for example, the following lines from the poem "It's the Layman," by Edgar A. Guest, quoted in a recent church bulletin in our possession (italics ours):

> Leave it only to the minister, and soon the church will die;
> Leave it to the *women*folk—the young will pass it by.
> For the church is all that lifts us from the coarse and selfish mob,
> And the church that is to prosper needs the lay*man* on the job.

III.
The Argument from the Nature of the Ministerial Office That Women Should Not Be Admitted to the Order of Ministry in the Church

A. A STATEMENT OF THE ARGUMENT

The complaint that the man, with God's supposed blessing, holds the ecclesiastical power of guardianship over the woman, brings us directly to the matter of ordination. As we have observed above, in the traditional discussion of the woman's right to the office of ministry the question of the nature of woman is always introduced in conjunction with the meaning of ordination, a matter to which we must now give attention.

In every major ecclesiastical tradition—Eastern Orthodox, Roman Catholic, and Protestant—it is recognized that there is an office of ministry and that ordination is the way in which one is inducted into that office. One is set apart for and enters upon the Christian ministry by way of ordination. However one may conceive of ordination—and there are differing theological viewpoints—there is a consensus that ordination is (ordinarily) necessary if one is to function as a minister in Christ's church with the authority of one divinely called to the task. Ordination constitutes, among other things, the church's confirmation of this divine call; and thus it certifies, as it were, one's right to serve as a minister of Jesus Christ.

Ordination presupposes, in other words, that there is a theological dimension to one's entry into the Christian ministry: one is "called" of God to the office; one does not simply choose to be a minister as one would choose to enter a profession. And this bears on the question of women's ordination. The question is, "Does God call women, as he does men, to be ministers in his church?" Those who are opposed to women's ordination answer, "Of course not." And they rebut the charge that this answer is obscurantist, in that emancipated women have excelled in all other professions, by pointing out that this very factor of calling means that the ministry cannot be equated *simpliciter* with a profession like medicine, law, or teaching.

This worthy and needed clarification, however, can hardly be the last word on the subject. Granted that the ministry differs from the professions in that only God can call a person to such a task, why should he call only men? Why should he not also call women? If, as C. S. Lewis protests, no one who opposes women's ordination is maintaining "that women are less capable than men of piety, zeal, learning and whatever else seems necessary for the pastoral office," then why, as Lewis himself puts it, should the church not draw "on the huge reserves which could pour into the priesthood if women were here, as in so many professions, put on the same footing with men?"[1]

Lewis responds to his own question by appealing to the character of the priestly office in the light of the larger question of the meaning of sexuality. The church, he reminds us, claims to be the bearer of revelation and, according to this revelation, sex is intended to illumine the hidden

[1]*God in the Dock* (Grand Rapids: Eerdmans, 1970), p. 234.

things of God. What the husband is to the wife, Christ is to the church. Hence the one who is invested with the ministerial office, which gives authority to minister in Christ's name, must be the one whom God has appointed to function at the natural level as husband and "head" of the family. Male and female, Lewis warns, are the "live and awful shadows of realities utterly beyond our control and largely beyond our direct knowledge." Hence, if we tamper with the basic functions God has assigned to each, we do so at our peril.[2] And this the church would be doing if it were to ordain to the sacred office of the ministry those for whom God intended another vocation in that he made them women.

Canon Geddes MacGregor also reasons in this manner, opposing as an American Episcopalian what Lewis opposed as a member of the Church of England. "Priesting women," as he calls it, has nothing to do with social and psychological considerations or else it would long ago have come to pass, along with the general movement of women's emancipation in modern society. If the argument is pitched on a psycho-sociological basis, then, indeed, the church is behind the times. But, says MacGregor, one cannot dismiss the practice of the church in this matter as an obscurantist commitment to mere custom. The fact that the *presbuteroi* of the New Testament, called *sacerdotes* by the time of Cyprian (*Ep.* 61), are always men indicates that the *semper ubique et ab omnibus* of tradition rests on "a radical theological reason." And what might this reason be? Just this: that the office of the Christian ministry derives from the ancient priestly office of the Hebrews. As it was unthinkable that a female should be a priest in Israel, so it is unthinkable that a woman should be a minister in the church, inasmuch as Christians are spiritual Levites and the church, the New Israel of God. And why was the Old Testament priestly function a male prerogative?

> Because God created man and woman to have different functions and the function of the male, which

[2]*Ibid.*, p. 239.

includes protection and guardianship of the family and home, is symbolized in the office of the priest who guards the temple and offers sacrifice.[3]

So far from being arbitrary or relative to changing social status, according to MacGregor, these functions are as inseparable from the male as is childbearing from the female.

In other words, the Christian ministry is proscribed to the woman because the meaning of her sexuality, as disclosed in the function given her by the Creator, is incompatible with the meaning of the ministerial office into which one is inducted by ordination. To ordain a woman to holy orders as a minister of Jesus Christ would be analogous to assigning her the role of fatherhood in the family.

This brings us a little closer to the heart of the matter. In the oldest tradition of the West, that of the Roman Catholic Church, and to a lesser degree in the Anglican tradition, ordination is a sacrament, involving an outward, visible sign, wherein is bestowed an inner, spiritual grace empowering one to perform the duties of the ministry. This grace is said to imprint on the recipient an "indelible character."[4] In the phrase "indelible character," the term "character" means the divinely given power or strength to perform the task of ministry.[5] This power is said to be "indelible" in

---

[3]"The Non-Priesting of Women: A Theological Consideration," *New Tracts for New Times*, 3:4. This tract for the times ends with the following salvo: "There is, in short, no inferiority or superiority hang-up in traditional Christian theology, but, rather, a pathological one among those who would infest the theological heritage of the church with the neuroses of a sick society in a bewildered decade of a not entirely undecadent age."

[4]Technically speaking, in the sacramental tradition, the phrase "receive the Holy Ghost," with what follows in the act of ordination, including the laying on of hands and the delivery of the Bible, imprints character (*characterem imprimit*) and confers the general faculties and powers of priesthood (*sacerdotii*) so that the one ordained has the right (*auctoritatem*) to offer public service to God and to exercise authority (*potestatem exerceat*) over the Christian people entrusted to his charge.

[5]This interpretation of priestly "character" is the minimal common meaning. There are those, to be sure, who construe it in terms of a metaphysical clericalism. But even for such it is at least the implantation of a spiritual potency (see Piet Fransen, "Orders and Ordination," *Sacramentum Mundi*, 4 [1969]:305–27).

the sense that it is given the ordinand once and for all in and through the sacrament of ordination. In other words, ordination, like baptism, is not to be repeated. In the sacramentalist tradition, then, the objection to the ordination of women takes the form of asserting that women are by nature incapable of receiving priestly "character." The ordination of a woman, in short, is an *impossibility*.

St. Thomas states this impossibility in terms of a *deficiency* which the woman suffers in spiritual receptivity and power, a rather shocking thesis to a modern reader. He cites female sexuality as impediment number one to receiving the sacrament of ordination, followed by such impediments, when found in the male, as defectiveness of reason, a state of servitude, the guilt of homicide, the stigma of illegitimacy, and the condition of physical mutilation.[6] Obviously such an approach assumes, as a kind of axiom, the inferiority of the woman. The functions or roles of the sexes rest upon an ontological hierarchy of worth and endowment.

As we have seen, modern opponents to woman's ordination eschew all suggestion that her incapacity to receive holy orders implies the woman's inferiority. The exclusion of the woman is a matter of her *difference from* the man rather than her *inferiority to* him, this difference being reflected in a difference of role. The woman is wife and mother while the man is husband and father. As such, the man is head and guardian of the home, a divinely given role in the natural family which must be reflected in the church, the spiritual family of God. In the current debate, in other words, Roman Catholics and Anglicans who oppose the ordination of women are following the tradition of the centuries in saying that woman, *per definitionem*, is incapable of receiving priestly or episcopal "character." Yet they insist that such incapacity implies no inferiority, as was assumed in other ages. What God has made woman to *be*, and what he intends for her to *do*, simply mark her as other than the man; they do not make her less than he.

[6]*Summa Theologica*, Supplement 29, 1.

B. A RESPONSE TO THE ARGUMENT

If one argues that the sexual role of the woman, in contrast to that of the man, excludes her from ordination, the argument does not seem to follow unless one supposes, as was traditionally the case, that such a role entails a deficiency of spiritual receptivity and power necessary to the office and task of ministry. Hence, if it is affirmed that there is no such deficiency—if the woman, who is created in the image of God as is the man, is admittedly capable of the same spiritual endowment, capable of the same "piety, zeal, learning and *whatever else* seems necessary for the pastoral office" (Lewis)—the argument that a woman cannot qualify for the ministerial office becomes problematical, to say the least. To take the position that a woman should not be admitted to the ministry, while conceding that she has the God-given capacity for it, is obviously to put oneself on a cleft stick.

And this is so, ultimately, whether one assumes a sacramentalist or an evangelical theology of ordination. The basic question is really not whether one speaks of a "sacrament" that conveys the "indelible character" of the "priesthood," or whether one repudiates the thought that ordination is a "sacrament" and refuses even to use the word "priest" to describe the Christian minister. All Christian churches teach in one way or another that God must give his enabling Spirit to those on whom hands are laid in ordination if they are to have the inner spiritual strength to serve him effectively as ministers of the church.[7] Therefore, to argue from the nature of ordination that women cannot hold the ministerial office implies that they are incapable of receiving that divinely given spiritual endowment symbolized by the laying on of hands in ordination.

---

[7]There are small groups of Christians (such as the Plymouth Brethren) who do not ordain anyone to the ministry in the traditional sense. They would constitute a kind of exception to the above generalization. In such groups, one sometimes hears ordination described as "empty hands on empty heads."

If one does not wish to say that this incapability is due to some inferiority in the woman, then what is the reason for it? The answer to this question comes as no surprise to those who are familiar with the literature: the woman's incapacity for ministerial orders is due to her subordination to the man in the God-ordained structures of life. This is why we have said that it ultimately does not matter whether one has a Roman Catholic view of ordination, in which the essential element is the sacramental commissioning of a priest to celebrate the sacrifice of the Mass, or whether one has a Protestant view, in which the essential element is the setting apart of a minister to preach the gospel and shepherd the people of God.[8] In both traditions it is the woman's relationship of subordination to the man that disqualifies her for ordination.

St. Thomas rejected female ordination as emphatically as anyone could. It is no more possible, he said, to have ordination without a *male* person than it is to have Extreme Unction without a *sick* person. But when he spells out why this is so, he gives the very same reason against the ordination of the woman that Luther and Calvin gave and that many of their followers still give. And it is the same reason which modern Anglicans give who appeal to the function of the male as the God-appointed "guardian and *head* of the family." Thomas's refutation of the plea that the female sex is no impediment to receiving holy orders begins with the affirmation:

> On the contrary, it is said (I Tim. 2:12), I suffer not a woman to teach (in the church, I Cor. 14:34) nor to

[8]We make this statement fully aware that the contrary has been frequently affirmed. "Arguments whether they [women] are capable of becoming Baptist or Congregational ministers or Calvinistic presbyters are, insofar as those ministries are conceived as being different from Holy Orders of the Catholic Church, very largely irrelevant . . ." (Mascall, "Women and the Priesthood of the Church," *Why Not? Priesthood and the Ministry of Women*, ed. Bruce and Duffield [Appleford: Marcham Manor Press, 1972], pp. 105f.). See below, pp. 74–97, for our analysis and comment on the Declaration, "Inter Insigniores," issued by the Vatican *contra* the ordination of women to the ministerial priesthood.

> use authority over the man. . . . *Since it is not possi-*
> *ble in the female sex to signify eminence of degree,*
> *for a woman is in a state of subjection, it follows*
> *that she cannot receive the sacrament of Orders. . . .*
> Wherefore, even though a woman were made the
> object of all that is done in conferring Orders [ton-
> sure, laying on of hands, etc.] she would not receive
> Orders. . . .[9]

The question of female ordination, then, is a nuance of the
larger question of female subordination. Whether one says
this in so many words, as does St. Thomas, or whether one
speaks of the man's function of procreation and guardianship in the family, it comes out to the same place. The
Christian minister is God's representative and the shepherd
of his flock, which is the church. And such a task implies a
spiritual authority which, by divine appointment, belongs to
the man and not the woman.

A thorough study of the larger question of sexual
hierarchy is not feasible at this juncture. As we indicated in
our introductory remarks, the position we espouse is one
which views the man/woman relationship as a partnership
in all of life, especially in the Christian church. And such a
theology of sexual partnership is wholly congruent with the
conclusion that there is nothing about ordination which
proscribes woman's entrance into the office of ministry.
Using the language of ordination to express such a theology
of partnership, one would say that in Christ there is a *uni-*
versal priesthood of *all* believers, female as well as male.

To this observation some have answered that Peter's
reference to Christians generally as a "holy" or "royal
priesthood" (I Pet. 2:5, 9) refers to the priesthood communi-
cated to the church in its *corporate* aspect. Hence the priesthood of *all* believers implies nothing for the ordination of
women to holy office unless one takes the Protestant view
of the church, which admits of no essential difference between laity and clergy. Given the radical laicism implied in

[9] *Summa Theologica*, Supplement 39, 1 (italics ours).

Protestantism, the only question to resolve, it is alleged, is the proper way of authorizing a layman to function as a clergyman and, in the case of a laywoman, the expediency of doing so. But for one who stands in the Catholic tradition, the problem with the ordination of women is one not of expediency but of theological principle, namely, the significant difference between the priesthood of the church as exercised by the laity (both men and women) and the priesthood of the church as exercised by individuals who are ordained as successors of the apostles and representatives of Jesus Christ.[10]

We shall deal more expressly with this argument—the supposed difference between the universal priesthood of all believers and the individual priesthood of the ministerial office—in due course.[11] For the time being we note only that even in the Catholic tradition, while it is not the whole truth, it is nonetheless a part of the truth that the "priestly character" committed individually by ordination to those who function as priests in the church arises out of the priestly character which is committed generally to the church as Christ's body. But if this is so—if the individual priesthood rests, to a degree, upon the general priesthood of the laity—then women, who, like men, are incorporated by baptism into the body of Christ and so made "to be priests unto his God and Father" (Rev. 1:6), are to this extent qualified to become priests in the individualized meaning of the

[10]This Catholic reading of Protestant theology is obviously not the whole story; for even when the "radical laicism" of Protestantism has been pressed, women have, one way or another, been made an exception to the rules by which men function. Witness, for example, Spener's eloquent—and for its day, historic—plea that *all* Christians have a right to expound Scripture as priests. To the question, "But do women also share in these priestly offices?" he answers, "Assuredly," and appeals to the fact that in Christ there is no male and female. Then follows the question, "But are women not forbidden to teach?" "Yes: *namely in the public congregation.* But that it is permitted to them outside the public congregation is clear from the passages and apostolic examples cited" (see Philip Spener, *The Spiritual Priesthood,* trans. A. G. Voigt [Philadelphia: The Fortress Press Society, 1917], Questions 60 & 61).
[11]See below, pp. 78ff.

term.[12] Whatever difference, then, one may postulate between the priesthood in its general and in its individual
form, this difference, we contend, should not be so stated as
to make the implications of the universal priesthood of all
believers radically different for the woman from what they
are for the man.[13] And so we are back where we began. The
argument that would exclude women from the ministry,
insofar as it rests on the nature of the ministerial office, is,
to us, unconvincing no matter how it is stated, because its
force really derives from the prior, unwarranted assumption
that the female sex cannot signify "the eminence of degree"
which the office of ministry implies, the woman being "in a
state of subjection" to the man.

ADDENDUM: CONCERNING PRIESTS AND PROPHETS

From time to time in the discussion of holy orders and the
woman's right to the same, the difference between the priest
and the prophet is mentioned. By remanding the discussion
of this matter to an addendum, we do not mean to imply
that this difference is of no consequence, but simply that it
appears to us of no consequence so far as the debate over
women in the ministry is concerned.

The prophet is one who speaks for God to the people
(cf. Heb. 1:11); the priest is one who speaks for the people to
God (cf. Heb. 5:1). The reason that this difference is sometimes mentioned with regard to women and the ministry is
not far to seek. The priesthood of the Old Testament was
strictly limited to males, as was the apostolate in the New.
In the Old Testament, however, some women were en-

---

[12]The Women's Ordination Conference, a Roman Catholic wom-
en's group, sells buttons proclaiming the unambiguous message, "Ordain
women or stop baptizing them" (see the *Los Angeles Times*, May 6, 1979,
Part VIII, p. 1).

[13]The same reasoning would apply, *mutatis mutandis*, to the consecration of women to the episcopal office, since all who are made priests in
Christ are also made kings (or a kingdom). See, again, Rev. 1:6: καὶ ἐποίησεν
ἡμᾶς βασιλείαν, ἱερεῖς τῷ θεῷ καὶ πατρὶ αὐτοῦ.

dowed with the gift of prophecy (II Kings 22:14); and at Pentecost the Spirit is said to have come not only upon sons but upon daughters as well (Acts 2:17–18), some of whom prophesied even in the assembled congregation (I Cor. 11:5). This being so, it becomes neccssary, if one believes women are not to receive ordination, to explain why the function of a prophet is compatible, while that of a priest is incompatible, with a woman's place in the church.

St. Thomas attempted to handle this problem by distinguishing between the "sacrament" of orders and the "gift" of prophecy. Since prophecy is not a sacrament but a charisma of God; and since the woman, "in matters pertaining to the soul," does not differ from the man; she can, he argued, receive the prophetic gift though she is not able to receive sacramental orders.[14] Such *ad hoc* reasoning hardly needs refutation, since it is an obvious *petitio principii.* Yet in the ongoing Catholic tradition, this Thomistic distinction between holy orders (priesthood) and divine gifts (prophecy), if not elaborated, is at least reflected in the tendency to associate the priesthood with the institutional side and prophecy with the charismatic side of the life of the church. However, it is commonly admitted, even by many Catholics, that ecclesiastical office and charisma cannot be neatly distinguished. Some would even go so far as to say that the priestly function in the church should be understood in the light of the prophetic rather than the cultic.[15]

In any case, whenever one tries to state it precisely, this argument that priests differ from prophets comes to grief so far as it is used to bar women from ordination. (This

[14]*Summa Theologica,* Supplement 39, 1.
[15]See Hans Küng, "Charism and Institution," *Why Priests?,* trans. Robert C. Collins (Garden City, N.Y.: Doubleday & Co., 1972), pp. 87–88. Also see Fransen, "Orders and Ordination," *Sacramentum Mundi,* 4:305–27. Of course, those who defend a male order of the priesthood would argue that the achievement of charismatic women (Catherine of Siena *et al.*) is no argument for their right to the ministry precisely because their achievement is charismatic. As such, it is veiled achievement, disclosing the inner meaning of creaturely cooperation with the divine, after the likeness of the Virgin's submission, and hence entirely within the boundaries of the woman's calling as bearer of the "eternal feminine."

may explain why St. Thomas simply affirmed the argument but refrained from elaborating it.) To illustrate, let us suppose, on the one hand, that one adopts the view of ministry which emphasizes that it is the individualized expression of the corporate *priesthood* of the church. In this case the minister is the one who, as an individual priest, speaks *to* God *for* the people. There is no evident reason for excluding women from doing this, since the church, as we have observed, includes women, and these women speak *to* God when they take part in corporate worship. In fact, if the church is the bride of Christ and therefore feminine to him, one could reason that the universal priesthood of the church should find its individual expression in the woman *rather than* the man. (Such reasoning would be at least as cogent as some of the arguments traditionally framed to exclude women from holy office.)

Let us suppose, on the other hand, that one adopts a view of ministry which emphasizes that it is the individualized expression of the *prophetic* tradition in the church. In this case the minister is the one who, as a prophet, speaks *for* God *to* the people. There is no reason for excluding women from doing this either, since, in the course of holy history, God has inspired prophetesses to speak in his name *to* his people, a fact to which Scripture plainly bears witness.

Of course an adequate theology of ministry would combine both of these perspectives. Whereas the Catholic tradition uses the word "priest" and the Protestant tradition, "minister," in both traditions the one who is ordained functions in worship both as a priest and as a prophet. He leads the congregation of God's people in the sacrifice of praise and petition addressed to God (priest) and in turn addresses them with a word from God (prophet). C. S. Lewis, with his usual precision of thought, observes this is so but then—impossible task—tries to draw a conclusion in favor of a male priesthood. Observing that he who leads the worship of the congregation is one who "represents us to God [priest] and God to us [prophet]," he goes on to say (speaking in terms of the Anglican liturgy),

> our very eyes teach us this in church. Sometimes the priest turns his back on us and faces the East—he speaks to God for us: sometimes he faces us and speaks to us for God. We have no objection to a woman doing the first: the whole difficulty is about the second.[16]

In other words, Lewis has no objection to women doing what *priests* do. The difficulty with women as *priests* surfaces when we think of their functioning as *prophets*! But this is how women, who were endowed with the prophetic gift, functioned in biblical times. Obviously this argument is somehow confused.

But though his argument may be confused, one should not overlook the point Lewis is making. If women were ordained to holy office, then a woman could stand in church before the congregation and do what men have always done. *She* would face us and *she*, with the authority residing in the divine word, would speak to us *for God*. This is "the whole difficulty" he is really alluding to, and to this difficulty we must now give our attention.

[16]*God in the Dock* (Grand Rapids: Eerdmans, 1970), p. 236.

IV.
The Argument That the Masculinity of God Entails a Male Order of Ministry in the Church

A. A STATEMENT OF THE ARGUMENT

1. Introduction

According to Scripture, the form or structure of our existence as human involves a fellowship of male and female (Gen. 1:27). For this reason humankind is redeemed as male and female; that is to say, the new humanity in Christ (his church) is made up of men and women who, as men and women, enjoy God and seek to glorify him. In the present discussion we shall assume—having argued the point in another place[1]—that this "I-thou" fellowship of man and woman is like the fellowship of the triune God, who is Father, Son, and Holy Spirit.

However, this likeness, this *analogia relationes,* as Barth calls it, between the human fellowship of male and female and the eternal fellowship of Father, Son, and Spirit,

---

[1]See my *Man as Male and Female* (Grand Rapids: Eerdmans, 1975), *passim.*

should not be pressed so as to suppose a sexual distinction in God. The theologians have always known and admitted as much, yet they have hardly been consistent in applying this truth. They have assumed that God is not female; but that God is not male either has been much less clear to them. It would be easy to attribute this inconsistency to their bias as men, and such a charge would by no means be unfounded. Yet there are other factors which obviously must be taken into consideration in accounting for the tendency of the theologians to think of God as a male Deity. For one, the Scripture uses predominantly masculine language in speaking of God. Furthermore, this God who reveals *him*self in Scripture as a *Father*, sent his *Son* to redeem humankind from their sins. This *Son*, in turn, became incarnate in the *man* Jesus of Nazareth. And this *man*, Jesus, appointed the original apostles to speak in his name, *all* of whom were *men*.

Surely it is understandable, if not defensible, that theologians should have inferred from all this that God is more like the male of the human species than like the female. Though the woman is in the divine image, it has been assumed that she is not in the image *to the same degree* as the man. (Some have said this expressly, some covertly and indirectly.) The woman is one degree removed from the original; she is "the glory of the man," who is "the image and glory of God" (I Cor. 11:7). By the same token it is surely understandable that Christian women have struggled with the implications of their faith at this point. Theresa of Avila's bitter lament has struck a responsive chord: "The very thought that I am a woman is enough to make my wings droop."[2] Today Christian women who study theology have lodged complaints against this male Deity of the theologians whose attributes reflect those qualities that our culture considers masculine and superior, qualities pecu-

---

[2]As quoted by Mary Daly, *The Church and the Second Sex* (New York: Harper and Row, 1968), p. 56. Here other passages are also cited in which the celebrated Spanish mystic and nun laments the privations of her sex, passages sometimes deleted from later editions of her original manuscript.

liarly applicable to the male of the species. Such a concept of the Deity they find more oppressive than redemptive, and not without reason.

Those who argue from the nature of God for the exclusion of women from the office of Christian ministry must, of course, demur to this complaint. For them it is not a matter of indifference that God is the "Father" who sent his "Son" as Redeemer and that both are referred to in Scripture and in Christian theology with the use of the masculine gender. Speaking to this point, E. L. Mascall observes:

> I do not suggest, of course, that there is in the Triune Godhead anything crudely corresponding to the biological characteristic of sex nor am I forgetful that in the book of Genesis God is described as creating both man and woman in his own image. Nevertheless, he created them in *his* own image, not in *hers*, and if it is suggested that the use of masculine terms is a mere accident of language or that the analogical application of terms to God is so remote that their gender is of no significance, it will, I think, be sufficient to remark that our belief in God would be different from what it is if the Trinity were described as consisting of Mother, Daughter and Spirit, or if, taking refuge in terms of common gender, we described it as consisting of Parent, Offspring and Spirit, simply.
>
> It is in no way derogatory to the female sex to point out that the Christian priest is to exercise fatherhood and not motherhood to God's family because his office is a participation in God's own relationship to his people and God is our Father in heaven and not our Mother. The female sex has its own peculiar dignity as we shall see in a moment, but we can hardly imagine it exercising the fatherhood of God. And that God is the Father of his people is one of the dominant themes of the Old and New Testaments alike.[3]

[3]"Women and the Priesthood of the Church," *Why Not! Priesthood and the Ministry of Women*, ed. Bruce and Duffield (Appleford: Marcham Manor Press, 1972), pp. 111–12.

"We can hardly imagine" the female sex "exercising the fatherhood of God." Underlying this reasoning is the thought that the officiating minister, whose task is to celebrate the Eucharist and preach the word to the worshiping community, does so for God and in *his* place. This masculine pronoun touches the crux of the matter. All agree that an ordained minister stands in God's place, and traditionally all have likewise agreed that to stand in *God's* place is to stand in a *masculine* place. Hence only a *man* may stand there.

C. S. Lewis sharpens the issues with a series of rhetorical questions. Can one, he asks, say that we might just as well pray to "Our Mother who art in heaven" as to "Our Father"? Dare one suggest that the Incarnation might just as well have taken a female as a male form and that the second Person of the Trinity be as well called Daughter as Son? Can one reverse the mystical marriage so the church is the bridegroom and Christ the bride? All this, he avers, is involved in the claim that a woman can stand in the place of God, as does a priest. Hence to admit women to the office of the ministry would be, for Lewis, to turn Christianity into a different sort of religion. Since Christians believe that God himself has taught us how to speak of him, we cannot look upon the masculine imagery of Scripture as unessential, merely human in origin. Even apart from the religious sphere, scholars have recognized the organic unity between image and apprehension, a unity as close as that of soul and body.

And though one may insist that women are equal with men—a thesis which Lewis allows with some effort— it does not follow, he reminds us, that the two are interchangeable, as though men could be wives, and women, husbands. In the spheres of the state, of economic and academic endeavor, we are concerned more with the human that is merely human, that is, with our own artifices. In these areas we feel free to shuffle and to experiment, for we are dealing with human beings more as "voters" and "hands." But in the church, which is the mystical bearer of revelation, the center rather than the periphery of our human reality is illuminated; or, to use another figure, we perceive the foundations on which our human reality rests.[4] Hence we are not free to alter the structures of our communal life in the church (as we are in the merely human orders of society) lest we jeopardize these very foundations.

2. The Incarnation

The argument that the masculine character of God entails a male order of ministry in his church is focused, theologically, in the doctrine of the Incarnation. According to this doctrine, Jesus is not simply another priest after the order of Aaron, nor simply another prophet, the last and greatest of those inspired men with a message from God. Rather, he is himself the eternal Son of God, who humbled himself, took upon himself the form of a servant, and was found in the likeness of men (Phil. 2:7). That is to say, in this man Jesus, who was a first-century Palestinian Jew, the eternal Son of God, whom Christians worship as Lord (John 20:28), was and is the acting Subject. This stupendous affirmation presupposes what theologians, when speaking of the Incarnation, have called the freedom of God, freedom to do what man the creature could never do, that is, step over the boundary which separates the creature from the Creator. Being human, the creature can never become God, but God the Creator can—and did—become human. But this mysterious freedom of God does not mean freedom to become human in some other way than as male or female. To suppose that God, as incarnate, partook of our humanity but not of our sexuality, as though he became neither male nor female, or both male and female, would be to deny his humanity. Since God made humankind male and female, if he were to become one of us he would have to become either a man or a woman. God had to make a choice, and the choice he made

---

[4]The argument I have here summarized, Lewis develops in an article entitled, "Priestesses in the Church?" reprinted in *God in the Dock* (Grand Rapids: Eerdmans, 1970), pp. 234f. (First published in 1948.)

is self-evident. Jesus of Nazareth was a man and not a woman, and to doubt this fact would be historical nonsense.[5]

Now those who argue from the nature of God as masculine to the conclusion that only men should be admitted to the office of the Christian ministry insist that the choice God made when he became incarnate reflects limitations imposed not only by our nature as human *but also by his nature as divine.* (This is a very crucial distinction for those who oppose women's ordination.) He who learned obedience as a Son (Heb. 5:8) was not only the son of Mary but the eternal Son of God. This is the ultimate reason why the incarnational union of the divine and the human in one person was a union of divinity and *male* humanity.

The Incarnation, it is further argued, is the prime paradigm of the way God intends the two sexes to be related in the church, because what happened in the Incarnation is uniquely extended in and through the church, which is the *Corpus Christianum.*[6] And precisely how are the sexes related in the Incarnation? The answer is obvious. It was a *male human nature* that the Son of God united to his divine Person; it was *a female human person* who was chosen to be his mother. On the other hand, no *male human person* was chosen to be the Messiah and no *female human nature* was assumed by a divine Person. Thus from one point of view the Incarnation exalts the male sex above the female, while from another point of view it exalts the female sex above the male. In no woman has human *nature* been raised to the dignity which it possesses in Jesus of Nazareth; and to no male human *person* has there been given a dignity compara-

[5]That Jesus was celibate is, of course, quite a different matter. It should also be noted at this point that the oft-made observation that Jesus reflects both "male" and "female" characteristics—such as severity and tenderness, strength and gentleness, maturity and childlikeness—simply means that he transcends and judges our sexual stereotypes, not our sexuality as such.

[6]The view that the church, in some sense, perpetuates what began in the Incarnation is virtually a theological axiom in the Roman and Anglo-Catholic traditions and has many more ramifications than are noted here. There is no need, however, to pursue these matters at this juncture.

ble to that which Mary enjoys as the mother of God, a dignity which, in the words of the Eastern Orthodox Church, makes her "more honorable than the cherubim and beyond comparison more glorious than the seraphim."[7]

This, then, is the difference between male and female in the economy of redemption, a difference so significant, it is argued, that it must be reflected in the ongoing life of the church. Those who argue in this manner seek to enhance the woman's place in the divine scheme of things by indicating how modern science has shown us that Mary's part in the Incarnation was vastly more significant than was possible to suppose using classic Aristotelian biology. No longer can the female's role in procreation be reduced to that of passive recipient. In fact, since Mary was a virgin, we now know that our Lord derived his humanity solely from his mother.[8] Yet for all that, the woman's place is obviously secondary.

3. The Male Apostolate

The supposed profound and mysterious meaning in the differentiation of male and female, focused in the Incarnation, explains (allegedly) why our Lord chose that the personal exercise of the ministry in his church should be restricted to male apostles. Being God's eternal Son, he became a man, not a woman; and for this reason he commissioned men to represent him in the church, which is his body, his bride.

[7]In the above summary of what may be called the "incarnational" argument for the different roles of male and female in the church, I have followed the statement of Mascall, "Women and the Priesthood of the Church," section 5, "Male and Female in Christianity." Whatever one may think of the argument, in fairness it should be noted that in no way does it require one to subscribe to the co-redemptrix doctrine of certain Roman Catholic Mariologists.

[8]Calvin, no less, found it necessary to reject the notion that since Jesus was born of a virgin, he "took his body out of nothing." He styles this position the error of the "new Marcionites who too haughtily contend that women are 'without seed.' Thus they overturn the principles of nature" (Institutes, II, xiii, 3). These "new Marcionites" sound to us like old male chauvinists who have achieved the reductio ad absurdum of their argument.

This appeal to Jesus' choice of an exclusively male apostolate fills out the traditional argument for limiting the office of ministry to men. To give the argument as much weight as possible, it is sometimes observed that the Gospels testify more clearly to Jesus' institution of the ministry than to his institution of the church. He founded the church, one might say, by founding a ministry. Hence the apostolic ministry, entrusted to men, is the rock on which the church is built.

The fundamental character of the ministry of the apostles is grounded in the fact that Jesus himself is the Apostle and High Priest of our confession, as the Epistle to the Hebrews says (3:1). As the one sent from God (*the* Apostle), he sends those who minister in his name (the *apostles*). As the one who sacrificed himself for sin and instituted the ritual expression of this sacrifice, namely, the rite of thanksgiving for bread and wine (*the* Priest), he commissions those who shall administer Holy Communion in his name (the *priests* or *presbyters*). Thus the ongoing ministry of Christ's church, derived from the apostles, is the task not only of the whole body (universal priesthood of all believers, I Pet. 2:5, 9; Rev. 1:6) but also and particularly of those who manifest their priesthood in that personal, individual form which the Lord has instituted in his church. We do not hear the word, nor are we baptized, nor do we celebrate the Eucharist, in an abstract way, but only as one ministers these benefits to us in Christ's name. And he who does this manifests Christ's priesthood in its inherent personal and individual character.[9]

The celebrant, then, in the liturgy of worship, acts both for our Lord Jesus Christ and for the One who sent him, who is God our Father. The vision of the heavenly worship in the Apocalypse (Rev. 4) reflects the inner reality of the liturgy of the church in that the central position is occupied

[9]It should be noted that this argument for limiting the ministerial office to men, as the successors of Jesus and the apostles, does not require any particular theory of apostolic succession. Of course, the more sacerdotal one's theology, whereby the grace of salvation is mediated *via* the priestly administration of the sacraments, the more important is the question of who shall function in the priestly office.

by the Father upon the throne and the Lamb in the midst thereof, flanked with the figures of the twenty-four elders, representing the twelve patriarchs of ancient Israel and the twelve apostles of the new Israel. Hence the minister, in the liturgy of the church, being the leader of the worshiping community on earth, must be a man as an instance of Christ and the Father in the worship of the redeemed in heaven.

And so, it is argued, one can see that to restrict the ministry to the male sex is a limitation congruous in every way with the basic truths on which the Christian faith rests. The example of our Lord in choosing only men as apostles, the pronouncements of Paul that women should keep silent in church (I Cor. 14) and not assume the teaching office (I Tim. 2:12), and the traditional practice of Christendom in limiting the ministry to men, must be understood from the perspective of these truths. The individual Christian priest (or minister) is ordained to represent the Head of the church, who is Jesus Christ. As a liturgical celebrant (to use the language of the Catholic tradition), the priest, when he presides over the Mass, does liturgically what Jesus the Lamb of God did historically when he offered up himself on the cross. As a herald of the gospel who proclaims the word (to use the language of the Protestant tradition), the minister, when he preaches the sermon, does liturgically what Jesus the Word of God did historically when he dwelt among us proclaiming the gospel of the kingdom and saying, "Repent, for the kingdom of heaven is at hand."

Hence the ultimate issue in both the Catholic and Protestant traditions, as far as women clergy are concerned, is that the clergy uniquely represents Jesus Christ; and Jesus Christ, the Lamb of God and the Word of God, was and is a man, not a woman. Therefore, a woman can never be given the authority to represent him in the church as gathered for worship. And because this is so, obviously the *onus probandi* lies with those who would simply set aside the common practice of the church as without significance in our day. The tradition of the church that only men should be ordained is surely more than mere tradition. Some have even said that it would take an ecumenical council, enlightened by a revelation of the will of God, to assume the responsibility of modifying what comes to us upon authority so mysterious and august.

B. A RESPONSE TO THE ARGUMENT

1. God and the Male Imagery of Scripture

In responding to the argument against the ordination of women derived from the being of God, we shall begin with the question, "What does the male imagery of Scripture imply for our understanding of the nature of God?" At first it might seem that the answer is obvious: God is "he," not "she." But if we take this answer to be unqualifiedly true, then we must say that God is more like a man than like a woman. The man is the primary manifestation of the image and glory of God; the woman is only secondarily so. From this conclusion there is no escape.

Contemporary theologians, perhaps for this reason, are less inclined than their predecessors unqualifiedly to draw this conclusion, as we have already noted. *Nonetheless, an affinity between maleness and divineness remains the basic assumption behind every argument from the nature of God for the exclusion of women from the office of the ministry.* The one who expounds the word, celebrates the sacraments, and shepherds the flock is the representative of God the Father, Jesus Christ his Son, and the Spirit, who bears witness to the Son in word and sacrament. This is why the word of the ministry was initially committed to male apostles; it is in its essential nature a male activity. For all the rhetoric about the peculiar dignity of the female sex, for all the protestation that the privilege which Christianity lays upon the male sex is a solemn responsibility and an awesome burden, for all the humble confession that most men are inadequate to fulfill the place belonging to them in the ministry, nonetheless to the male belong the privilege and the responsibility and the dignity in God's church, because God is a masculine Deity.

But if, as theologians have always taught, there is only a "personal" distinction in God (Trinity), not a "sexual" one, then the creation of humankind in the divine image as male and female can hardly mean that God is male and *not* female. As we have already observed, if God is a fellowship of Persons (Father, Son, and Holy Spirit), and the human creature a fellowship of persons (male and female), then humanity is like God as man *and* woman rather than as man *in distinction from* woman. This conclusion is as obvious as the noonday sun. But then, what of the linguistic usage of Scripture? Is the masculine language of the Bible simply the product of the patriarchal, male-dominated, Semitic culture of Israel, taken over uncritically by the church? Does it really matter whether we say "he" or "she," "Father" or "Mother," "Son" or "Daughter," when speaking of God?

Those who confidently respond to this last question: "Yes, it does matter!" often cite the Old Testament proscription of the fertility cults. As we seek an answer to our question, therefore, let us begin by looking at certain data in the Old Testament. It is a well-known fact that goddesses, especially mother goddesses, were worshiped in the fertility cults of Canaan and the world surrounding ancient Israel. And it cannot be doubted that whenever the Israelites indulged in these pagan rites, it provoked a vehement protest from the reforming prophets. In both Amos and Hosea there are scathing denunciations of the widespread practice of ritual prostitution associated with Canaanite fertility cults (Amos 2:7f.; Hosea 4:14f.). And Jeremiah is told not to intercede for a people who worship the "queen of heaven" (Ishtar). Whole families participated in this worship; the children gathered the wood, the fathers kindled the fire, and the women kneaded the dough for the cakes. And this they did, not shamefacedly, but brazenly, in the cities of Judah, in the very streets of Jerusalem (Jer. 7:16ff.). Even the remnant of Judah that fled to Egypt defied the prophet, saying they would continue to pour out libations to the queen of heaven as their mothers and fathers before them had done and as the kings and princes of Judah had also done (Jer. 44:15ff.). Asherah, the female counterpart of Baal, seems to have been especially attractive to ancient Israel. Her cult image was set up in Jerusalem (I Kings 15:13) and Samaria (I Kings 16:33; II Kings 13:6; 21:3), and during Manasseh's reign her image stood in the temple of the Lord himself in Jerusalem (II Kings 21:7).

Yet there is no evidence that this worship of female gods was more offensive to the prophets than the worship of other deities. It is the worship of *false* gods, not *female* gods as such, that is the ultimate abomination to the Lord. The gulf is just as deep between the worship of Baal and Jahweh as it is between the worship of Asherah and Jahweh. Women, to be sure, are prominently mentioned in the worship of goddesses—Asa removed his own mother from being queen because of the image she made to Asherah (I Kings 15:13). But one can hardly see any more in all this than one sees in the frequent mention of *men* who participated in the worship of false *gods*. (This same good King Asa put *male* cult prostitutes out of the land and removed the idols his *fathers* had made, I Kings 15:12.) It surely seems a bit pejorative, therefore, to confront the argument for women in the Christian ministry with the observation that the devotees of false religions have had their goddesses who were mothers, and priestesses who were cultic prostitutes.[10] The most that can be said is that the survival of fertility cults and the worship of mother goddesses in Israel may have reinforced the male imagery which dominates the worship of Israel's God, whose name is

---

[10]C. S. Lewis, speaking against the proposal to allow women in the priesthood of the Church of England, observes, "Goddesses have, of course, been worshiped; many religions have had priestesses. But they are religions quite different in character from Christianity" (*God in the Dock*, p. 237). One could just as well say, "*Gods* have been worshiped; many religions have had *priests*. But they are religions quite different in character from Christianity."

Jahweh. And this male imagery, of course, was compatible with the male priesthood already firmly established by the patriarchal culture of the Hebrew people.

As for male imagery, it is obvious that the Israelites of the Old Testament thought of Jahweh principally in male categories. He is the God of battle who delivered them from the Egyptians, the Amorites, and the Moabites. "Lord of hosts," i.e., armies, is a common designation of the God of Israel (I Sam. 1:3, 11). He is not only a warrior, but also a husband whose wife is Israel (Isa. 54:5); and more especially, he is a Father whose son is Israel (Mal. 1:6; 2:10). But in this very language there is a hint, too often overlooked, that the reality corresponding to the imagery is lost, or at least misunderstood, if one takes such language literally. Israel cannot *literally* be related to God both as wife and as son. But if one admits as much, if one acknowledges that these terms describe the intimately personal and unique relationship of Israel to God under the figures of a wife (female) and of a son (male) because both can serve to illumine a truth which neither, taken by itself, is adequate to accomplish, *then one should be prepared to admit the same possibility of God.*

It is true, of course, on the divine side, that both the husband and the father figures are male. Yet in the Old Testament there are some references to God in terms of female imagery. In Numbers 11:12 Moses complains, "Did *I* conceive all this people? Did *I* bring them forth that thou shouldst say to me, 'Carry them in your bosom as a nurse carries the sucking child to the land which you did swear to give their fathers?'" Obviously this rhetorical question is meant to convey the idea of the preposterous. But that which is preposterous is that *Moses* rather than *God* should be shouldered with the responsibility for Israel. The incongruity is heightened, to be sure, by the use of the maternal, female imagery, since Moses the lawgiver is a man, not a woman. But there is nothing preposterous in the thought that *God* should assume the ultimate responsibility for Israel because of the relationship he sustains to his people, a relationship as intimate as that of mother and nursing child.

Since the Lord is the one who "conceived" Israel, let the Lord "carry them in *her* bosom as a nurse carries a sucking child" in hers.

And there are other places in the Old Testament which use such maternal language of God. One such place is found in the Song of Moses, this same male lawgiver. In this passage Israel's unfaithfulness is rebuked in the line, "You were unmindful of the Rock that bore you, and you forgot the God who gave you birth" (Deut. 32:18). The fact that translators have given this text as male a rendering as possible tells us more about the sex of the translators than about the nature of God.[11] Similar language occurs in one of the closing visions of the book of Isaiah. Speaking of the blessings of the Messianic age in the maternal image of bountiful breasts (66:11), the word of the Lord by the prophet likens Jerusalem to a mother whose sucklings are carried on her side and dandled on her knees (66:12). This motherly act of Jerusalem leads to a promise of a motherly act on God's part (v. 13): "As one whom his mother comforts, so I will comfort you; and you shall be comforted in Jerusalem." Here the masculine is used of Israel (*his* mother) and the feminine of God (his *mother*).

Perhaps the most moving passage of all, and certainly

[11]The first verb, יָלַד, may mean "beget," as Cush "begot" Nimrod (Gen. 10:8), but its common connotation is "to bear," "to bring forth." The second verb, חוּל, "to writhe," "to twist," in the pain of childbirth, can only be maternal in meaning. Hence to translate, "You were unmindful of the Rock that begot you, and you forgot the God who fathered you" (New Jerusalem Bible), or the "Rock that begat thee . . . the God that formed thee" (KJV), is really indefensible. It imposes male imagery on female language in the one instance and neutralizes it in the other. See the *Los Angeles Times*, May 12, 1973, Part 1, p. 23, on feminist protest to such arbitrary translation procedures.

Such scholarly bias pales to insignificance, however, beside the chauvinist translations found in some contemporary speech versions. Jesus said (Luke 15:10) that the repentance of a sinner brings joy to the angels. According to *Living Letters*, so does the veil on a submissive woman's head: "So a woman should wear a covering on her head as a sign she is under man's authority, a fact for all the angels to notice and rejoice in" (I Cor. 11:10)! (The Greek simply says—rather enigmatically—that the woman should have [the sign of] authority on her head *on account of* the angels, διὰ τοὺς ἀγγέλους.)

one of the most lofty, is Isaiah 49:15: "Can a woman forget her sucking child, that she should have no compassion on the son of her womb? Yea, she may forget, yet will I not forget you." Calvin comments as follows:

> By an appropriate comparison he shows how strong is his anxiety about his people, comparing himself to a mother, whose love toward her offspring is so strong and ardent as to leave far behind it a father's love. Thus he did not satisfy himself with proposing an example of a father (which on other occasions he very frequently employs), but in order to express his very strong affection, he chose to liken himself to a mother and calls them not merely "children," but the *fruit of the womb*, towards which there is usually a warmer affection. What amazing affection does a mother feel toward her offspring, whom she cherishes in her bosom, suckles on her breast and watches over with tender care so that she passes sleepless nights, wears herself out by continued anxiety and forgets herself![12]

Calvin, it may be, like other commentators after him, waxes eloquent over this Scripture because God only *likens* himself to a mother, using a figure that is obviously not to be taken literally. By contrast, in many passages in the Old Testament God is not only *likened* to a father, but is said to *be* a Father. As the same prophet, Isaiah (63:16), says, "For thou art our Father, though Abraham does not know us and Israel does not acknowledge us." Indeed, God himself calls himself a Father: "A son honors his father, and a servant his master. If, then, I am a Father, where is my honor? . . . says the Lord of hosts to you, O priests, who despise my name" (Mal. 1:6).

2. The Analogical Nature of Such Imagery

Yet surely we cannot infer from such masculine language, frequent and natural though it be, that it implies any more than that God is *like* a father. In other words, *the Old Tes-*

---

[12]*Commentary on Isaiah* (Grand Rapids: Eerdmans, 1948), 4:30–31.

tament speaks in the same sort of analogical way about God when the language is paternal as when it is maternal. Although the former is much more frequent, the frequency does not change the quality of the statements. All such statements which liken God to a father or a mother are possible because "God created Man in his image." And this creature, who is in the image and likeness of God, is male and female. In other words, when the Old Testament likens God to a father or mother, the language used is analogical in both instances. And the univocal element in the analogy is not our likeness to God (or God's likeness to us) as male *in contrast to* female, but as male *and* female. That is to say, using the words of the Old Testament itself, God is like a father who pities his children (Ps. 103:13) and a mother who cannot forget her sucking child (Isa. 49:15). And both analogies are equally revelatory because humankind as male *and* female is like God.[13]

Since it is true that God is like a father and like a mother, one can understand how Jesus, though he spoke of God as his Father and taught his disciples to address God in prayer as "Our Father," could liken God to a woman, which no rabbi had ever done. Between the familiar parables of the lost sheep and the lost son (Luke 15:1–7, 11–32) is the parable which tells of a woman who lights a lamp and sweeps her whole house till she finds what she had lost (Luke 15:8–10). In this parable the woman stands for God. God, then, is not only like a shepherd who seeks a lost sheep, or a father who welcomes home a lost son, but also like a woman who rejoices with her friends and neighbors when a lost coin is found.[14]

[13]Phyllis Trible argues that the Old Testament speaks of Jahweh not only as nurse and mother, but also as midwife, housekeeper, and seamstress ("Depatriarchalizing in Biblical Interpretation," *Journal of the American Academy of Religion*, XLI, 1, 41 [1973]:30–48).

[14]See below, p. 54, note 25, for futher comment on the interpretation of this parable. In this regard, it should be noted that whereas a yearling *male* lamb or goat answers in type to Jesus, our Passover, sacrificed for us (cf. Ex. 12:5–6; I Cor. 5:7), yet our Lord likened himself to a *hen* who gathers *her* chicks under *her* wings (Matt. 23:27).

One is reminded here of the usage of the apostle Paul when speaking of his own ministry, usage which is all the more striking in view of his decided patriarchal leanings. Paul was a male who probably thought God was more like a man than a woman (the man [ἀνήρ] "is the image and glory of God," I Cor. 11:7); yet, he describes himself, in his apostolic role, both as a male and as a female. We are familiar enough with the masculine imagery he uses, as when he reminds his Corinthian converts that though they have had many teachers in Christ, they have only one father. "I," he says, "became your father in Christ Jesus through the gospel" (I Cor. 4:15). But he also uses other figures. In the first letter he ever sent to a group of converts, he reminds them that he became gentle among them like a nurse (τροφός) who cherishes her children (I Thess. 2:7). And some years later, when he writes to the Galatians, distressed at the news that had reached him, he uses very graphic female language of himself. Calling them his children, he wonders out loud if he had really brought them to birth, as he had supposed when present with them. Could it be that he was deceived, that he was like a woman who had had false labor pains? "My little children," he writes, "with regard to whom I am again in travail until Christ be formed in you!" (Gal. 4:19). The verb used (ὠδίνω) describes the pangs of a woman caught in the throes of a difficult and painful birth.

Of course he might have spoken quite as appropriately—though in this case surely not as effectively—in the imagery of fatherhood. But that is just the point: either form of speaking to his converts, whether as a father or as a mother, would have been equally appropriate because the relationship which he had to them was illumined by both the father role and the mother role. And this is true because God, whose emissary he was, is both like a father and like a mother in relating to his people.

Now if the Bible likens God to both a father and a mother, this implies that in his own being God is also *un*like either, since all analogies are comparisons with a difference. A human father's pity for his children and a human

mother's care for her infant discloses to us not only something of what God is like, but also something of what he is
not like. The difference between Man and God in this regard
is that human fatherhood and human motherhood presup-
pose a sexual distinction between male and female. Because
of this distinction, at the creaturely level a male can be only
a father, and a female, only a mother. But unlike us, God can
be both a Father and a Mother to his people; he is not subject
to the either/or of fatherhood or motherhood as we are.[15]
That is to say, God is like a human father, *not* in his sexuality as a male, but in the pity which he shows for his children; and God is like a human mother, *not* in her sexuality
as a female, but in the solicitude which she shows for the
well-being of her infant offspring.

In other words, God's mode of personal existence
transcends sexual distinctions—as the theologians have always known and admitted. Hence they have been palpably
inconsistent with themselves when they have inferred from
the male imagery used of God in Scripture that he is masculine in his nature and not feminine. Logically they might
just as well have inferred from the female imagery used of
God in Scripture that God is feminine and not masculine.
The long and the short of it is that if God transcends human
sexual distinctions in his essential being, then one cannot
predicate of him either masculinity or femininity in the
human sense of the terms. To be sure, the trinitarian names
of "Father," "Son," and "Spirit" show grammatical gender.
The word for "father," both in Hebrew and in Greek, is
masculine, as is the word for "son." But this no more implies the masculinity of the first and second Persons in the
Trinity than the feminine Hebrew word for "spirit" (רוּחַ) or
the neuter Greek word (πνεῦμα) implies the femininity or
neuterness of the third Person of the Trinity. It is high time,
then, that theologians stopped making statements like,

---

[15]Here Bunyan's quaint portrait of the Holy Spirit comes to mind:
"The man whose picture this is, is one in a thousand; he can beget children, travail in birth with children, and nurse them himself when they are
born."(!) *The Pilgrim's Progress*, ch. V.

"God is, of course, masculine, but not in the sense of sexual
distinction." Mary Daly quotes this remark of J. L. McKen-
zie, S.J., and comments tellingly, "This is the sort of nonsense statement which philosophers of the linguistic
analysis school delight in dissecting."[16]

But one may still have a sense of ambivalence as one
struggles with the issue of how to speak of God. Theologians
teach that God transcends the sexual distinction that marks
our creaturely fellowship as male and female, yet they have
always said that *he* transcends this distinction, never *she*.
When speaking of God, they have deemed it necessary to say
he is neither male nor female and improper to say *she* is
neither male nor female. Indeed, all our language about God,
not only the language of theology but especially the language of worship and devotion—the litanies offered, the
hymns sung, the sermons preached—reflects a universal

---

[16]*The Church and the Second Sex*, p. 139. The literature on wom-
en's ordination abounds with similar statements. Consider the following by
former episcopal bishop C. Kilmer Myers of California:

> In the imagery of both the Old and New Testaments God is
> represented in masculine imagery. The Father begets the Son. This
> is essential to the *givenness* of the Christian Faith, and to tamper
> with this imagery is to change that Faith to something else. [But]
> this does not mean God is a male, [for] biblical language is the
> language of analogy. It is imperfect, even as all human imagery of
> God must be imperfect. Nevertheless, it has meaning. The male
> image about God pertains to the divine initiative in creation. Initia-
> tive is, in itself, a male rather than a female attribute.... The
> generative function is plainly a masculine kind of imagery, making
> the priesthood a masculine conception ("Should Women Be Or-
> dained?" as quoted in "Women and the Language of Religion," *The
> Christian Century*, April 14, 1976, p. 356).

In this paragraph, matters momentarily take a hopeful turn for the
woman, inasmuch as the imagery of God as Father and Son is affirmed to be
imagery only, not literal reality. "God is not a male." But then comes the
inevitable twist. Since God is *masculine* and the priesthood a *masculine*
conception, concludes the bishop, *women*, who are feminine, cannot be
priests. So in the end, "masculine" means *male* after all. The term slides
under his hand; and when the good bishop is through with his statement, he
has had his cake and eaten it too. His doctrine of God is orthodox in its
traditional inclusion of women, and his doctrine of the priesthood is secure
in its traditional exclusion of them. A language which enables one to do
this is, indeed, a useful and powerful instrument—if one is a man in both
the generic and the specific sense at the same time.

consensus: the proper way to speak of God is in the masculine gender. And it is not simply a matter of propriety thus to speak; God himself, in his self-revelation in the Bible, has taught us so to speak. Hence we find it difficult to realize the limitations of such habitual, elementary usage. If "he" does not mean "he," a layperson might ask, what does it mean?

In answer to this question it should be observed that just as the masculine noun "man" may be used of human persons generally, not simply of a male human person specifically, so the personal pronouns "he," "him," and "his" may have a general meaning as well as a specific one. When they use such personal pronouns of God, the theologians have always understood them to have a generic meaning only, not a specific one. To speak grammatically, "he" is used of God as a *personal* pronoun, not a *masculine* personal pronoun. The real issue, then, behind this usage is the *personal* character of God. It is essential to Christian piety that God be addressed as "Thou" in contrast to the impersonal Absolute, the Ground of Being of religious philosophy. The God of the Bible and of Christian piety is not an "It," a neuter, but the God who says, "I am who I am" (Exod. 3:14). And this personal divine "I" is to be addressed as Subject. He is the God to whom we pray, saying, "Hallowed be *thy* name; *thy* kingdom come, *thy* will be done." Since the one true God is a personal God, we must speak *to* him as "Thou"; and for the same reason, we speak *about* him as "he," in both instances employing the singular of the *personal* pronoun. To refer to God as "he" should mean only that God is a personal God in contrast to an abstract, philosophic idea.[17]

To refer to God as "she," on the other hand, given

---

[17]It is the need to avoid the abstract, impersonal "It" when referring to God that explains why we have traditionally spoken of the Holy Spirit in the masculine, in keeping with the received doctrine of the church which designates the Spirit as one of the *hypostases* of the Godhead, even though the Greek πνεῦμα is neuter. But see the addendum, "The Holy Spirit as Female(?)," pp. 47–54. For further comment on the use of the masculine "he" in the generic sense and the problems with such usage, see the Introduction to Section VI, pp. 119–23.

received linguistic usage, would mean not only that God is personal but that God is female, since the feminine personal pronoun does not have a generic, but only a specific, connotation. Hence to use the feminine personal pronoun in speaking of God would obscure the truth about him, in a way that the use of the masculine personal pronoun need not do. Nevertheless, the pronoun "he," when used of God, *may*, indeed, obscure the truth about him and, as a matter of fact, *has* done so. And why do we say this? Because men have found it—*without* good reason—well-nigh impossible to remember that when used of God in Scripture, "he" is a *personal*, not a *masculine*, pronoun, with the result that women—*with* good reason—are finding it increasingly difficult to accept this same distinction. Thus the *latent* distortion on the lips of insensitive males is now becoming an *evident* distortion to the ears of sensitive females.

We say that good reason is on the women's side because women have just as much right to think that God is like themselves as do men, for they are persons in the divine image even as men are persons in the divine image. And this little exercise in language analysis shows how far off the mark is the argument of those who oppose women's ordination because of the linguistic usage of Scripture. It is the women who are seeking ordination, not the men who are opposing them in it, who have the most reason to talk about biblical language. Even if women, in advocating their right to the office of the ministry, affirm (as some, though not many, do) that we should say "she" not "he," "Mother" not "Father," "Daughter" not "Son," when speaking of God, at worst are they not simply confronting an age-old distortion with a new one? And it ill becomes those who are guilty of an old distortion simply to cite its hoary pedigree against those who would replace it with a new one.

In any event, to say that God is equally like man and woman, hence men and women are equally qualified to speak for him as his ministers, is not to change Christianity into some other religion; it does not even require that we change biblical usage as such. It remains proper to speak of

God as "he." But it is not only proper but *necessary* that we strive for precise understanding of what such usage implies and what it does not imply about the nature of God. In fact, we must strive for more than precise understanding. What is needed is the *redemption* of such usage. And that redemption can take place only when men relate to women in such a way that "he" does not symbolize "her" oppressor, but "her" partner. Then, and only then, will "he" truly be the proper way to speak of God. And until such redemption is a reality, we must be open to those possibilities for change latent in all living languages. In the Epilogue, "Theology and the Language of the Masculine," we will explore some of these possibilities for change, with special attention to the question of biblical language. But now a word about the Holy Spirit as female.

ADDENDUM: THE HOLY SPIRIT AS FEMALE (?)

In commenting on the male imagery with which Scripture speaks of God, we have argued that God is not a Father literally, as are human fathers who are males; nor is God a Son literally, as Jesus was literally the son of Mary. But what of the Holy Spirit? As everyone knows, theologians have traditionally spoken of God as "he"; and, since this God is Father, Son, and Holy Spirit, they have used the same pronoun, "he," when speaking of the third Person of the Godhead, whose specific trinitarian name is "the Holy Spirit." In this addendum we wish to comment briefly on this usage.

Since the Greek πνεῦμα ἅγιον is neuter, and since the word "spirit" can be equated with "energy," "force," or "influence," there has been a tendency on the part of Christians to think of the Holy Spirit as an "it." When speaking of the Spirit, therefore (in distinction to the Father and the Son), our language problem is somewhat different. Rather than remind ourselves that the pronoun "he" is personal (generic), not masculine (specific), we have had to remind ourselves that the pronoun "he" is not neuter; i.e., we have had to remind ourselves that when we speak of the Spirit as "he," we use the personal pronoun in contrast to the impersonal pronoun, and thereby affirm that the Spirit is a Person (*hypostasis*) in the Godhead.

There are those, as we have noted, who would go further and suggest that actually the Holy Spirit is the *feminine* personal principle in the Godhead and that were this truth reinstated in our theology, as it ought to be, we should then have a more balanced view of God. Then we would overcome the problem of a masculine Deity made in the image of the male theologians who always speak of God as "he" rather than "she." (At the beginning of this book we have reproduced a fresco, found in a small Bavarian church, portraying the Holy Spirit as a woman. With breasts clearly shown, "she" stands between two men, the Father with white hair and beard on her right and the Son with brown hair and beard on her left.)

As for this notion that the Holy Spirit may be thought of as female, Jerome (A.D. 340–420) is the first prominent scholar to mention it. In his commentary on Isaiah, he expresses surprise that in the apocryphal *Gospel According to the Hebrews*, the Spirit is a female. He had in mind the saying attributed, in this Gospel, to Jesus: "Then my Mother, the Holy Spirit, seized one of my hairs and bore me away to the high mountain of Tabor." A doxology, found in another apocryphal work, *The Acts of Thomas*, concludes with the words, ". . . and the Holy Spirit, the Mother of all creation." Both of these apocryphal works are late second- or third-century documents, belonging to the rubric of romance rather than history and employing legendary materials to supplement the canonical accounts of Jesus' life and that of his disciple, Thomas.

In the Near East, at the time of the planting of the Christian church by the apostles and their successors, there were many cults involving the worship of goddesses; and it has been suggested that before the rise of the veneration of Mary as the Mother of God, it would have been relatively easy to confuse the Holy Spirit with one of these mother goddesses, especially since in Aramaic and Syriac, as in Hebrew, the word for "spirit" (רוּחַ) is feminine. It also appears that among certain Gnostic sects the Spirit was identified with the Mother Principle. (The Mandaeans and the Ophites called the Spirit "the first woman" and "Mother of all living.") In the West, according to Hippolytus, the Valentinians interpreted the Spirit, appearing in the form of a dove at Jesus' baptism, as "the word of the Mother from above," that is to say, of Wisdom (*Sophia*). Hippolytus, of course, seeks to refute these and other Gnostic sects, some of whom, he says, refer to the Spirit as a "virgin." Authorities in Gnostic speculation (as, for example, Bousset) are confident that the female companion of Simon Magus (featured in the third- and fourth-century pseudo-Clementine literature and named "the Holy Spirit") is to be identified with the moon goddesses Isis, Astarte, and Aphrodite.

Turning from these obscure and heretical sects on the periphery of the Christian church to the mainstream of Christianity, we find virtually nothing to indicate that the church ever accepted these speculations about the female character of the Holy Spirit. Peter Gerlitz, on whose research we have mainly depended for the above information, is confident, however, to have found evidence that early (ante-Nicene) Christian thought about the Spirit shows "traces" of speculation related to beliefs in oriental mother-goddesses.[18] But his evidence appears to us, for the most part, rather tenuous. While it may be that Hippolytus sought to find the Trinity in the Old Testament by allegorizing the story of Isaac, Jacob, and Rebecca in a way that made Rebecca a type of the Holy Spirit; and while it may also be that the prayer of the officiating priest to the "Mother of spiritual children" appearing in an obscure Syrian baptismal liturgy could be construed as a prayer to the Holy Spirit (assuming some sort of identity between Wisdom [*Sophia*] and the Spirit); how much weight can be placed on such data? It is granted that the Spirit is represented as a dove in

[18]*Ausserchristliche Einflüsse auf die Entwicklung des christlichen Trinitatsdogmas* (Leiden: E. J. Brill, 1963), pp. 120ff.

Jesus' baptism and that in Gnostic speculation Wisdom personified as female (*Sophia*) has a prominent role. But can one say that the dove symbolism of the Gospel account reflects an affinity with this Wisdom symbolism of Gnosticism? Again, it is granted that in the thought of the early Fathers, the church is sometimes likened to a mother, a thought which becomes ever more secure with the passage of time. But is it really obvious, even plausible, that they spoke thus because they thought of the church in terms of an oriental mother-goddess? And even if there were such an affinity of thought—which we doubt—in their ecclesiology, would it imply that the Holy Spirit is a motherly Spirit because the church, as female, is implicitly the bearer of the Spirit?

Gerlitz entitles a section of his research in which these arguments are found, "Traces of Oriental Mother-Goddesses in the Spirit Speculation of Early Christianity." His opening sentence is the confident affirmation: "That רוּחַ [spirit] in Hebrew was thought of as feminine can be seen already in Gen. 1:2 where it is said of the Spirit 'He [sic] brooded over the waters.' Hence the Spirit of God, who shares in the creation of the world, is female."[19] It were better to be a little less certain and thus a little more accurate and observe that in the common translation of this text, the Spirit of God is set forth in the figure of a bird hovering over the nest. That is to say, this is a passage of Scripture where God is spoken of as Spirit in the figure of a bird which *may* be understood as a female of the species. So far as the Old Testament is concerned, to use such a female figure for God is uncommon, but not necessarily unique.[20]

It is true that the divine Wisdom or Energy by which

[19]*Ibid.*, pp. 127–28.

[20]As we have already observed, the feminine gender of the Hebrew רוּחַ is no more significant for our inquiry than the neuter gender, already alluded to, of the Greek πνεῦμα. Both mean "spirit," yet obviously the Spirit of God cannot be both feminine and neuter. This simply illustrates the pedantry of those who seek to resolve problems, supposedly of the dogmaticians' making, by erudite appeals to etymology, grammar, and syntax.

The reason Gerlitz can read so much into the feminine gender of רוּחַ is that he assumes that the Gnostic understanding of the dove symbolism in the baptism of Jesus, as being female symbolism, was shared by

God creates and rules the world, a Wisdom which eludes Man in his overweening search for understanding (Job 28:12f.), is personified in the book of Proverbs as female. She is begotten before all things as God's architect and counselor in creation (Prov. 8:22–31); she builds a palace and spreads a feast for those who will receive her instruction (9:1f.); she teaches in public places (1:20; 8:1ff.); she gives her pupils the divine Spirit (1:23); and by her discipline the simple become wise, rulers rule wisely, and those seeking her are richly rewarded (8:14–21).[21]

Anyone familiar with Christian thought will perceive that what the sage in the book of Proverbs describes as the work of divine Wisdom, personified as a female, is, in the New Testament, primarily the work of Jesus Christ, who obviously was a male. As Wisdom is the counselor of God in creation, so he is the Logos who is with God in the beginning, through whom all things are made (John 1:2–3). And as *she* gives instruction, grants understanding, and bestows the divine Spirit; so our Lord, in the exercise of *his* prophetic office, teaches with authority, likening those who heed his words to the *wise* who build on a rock in contrast to the foolish who build on the sands of their own understanding (Matt. 7:24–27). It is also noteworthy that the saying of Jesus (Matt. 23:34), "Wherefore behold *I* send to you prophets . . . ," is reported in Luke (cf. 11:49) as "Wherefore also the *Wisdom* [Greek feminine, σοφία] of God says, 'I will send to you prophets'. . . ." In the same vein is the Pauline affirmation that to those who are called, both Jews and Greeks, Christ is

---

the ancient church of the East. But the evidence for this conclusion is far from convincing. Nor is it intrinsically necessary, since there are (one may assume) as many male as female doves. When Watts, for example, teaches us to sing,

Come Holy Spirit, heavenly Dove,
With all thy quickening powers,

given *his* theology, he probably was thinking of a male dove. Correct theology would allow us to think of either a male or a female dove as we sing this hymn because God, as Spirit, is like *both* as well as unlike *either*.

[21]See F. Brown, S. R. Driver, and C. A. Briggs, *A Hebrew and English Lexicon of the Old Testament* (Oxford: Clarendon Press, 1906), under חכמה.

the "*wisdom* of God" (I Cor. 1:24); for they are in Christ Jesus, who has been made to them "wisdom from God, both righteousness and sanctification and redemption . . ." (I Cor. 1:30). Since he is the One in whom, for Christians, are hid all the treasures of wisdom and knowledge (Col. 2:3), it is obvious that the feminine gender of both the Hebrew and Greek words for "wisdom" had, for the writers of the New Testament, no particular significance. Even the hypostatizing of Wisdom as a female in the proverbs of Israel was no impediment to their viewing Jesus as the ultimate revelation and true personification of this divine Wisdom.

Leaving the specifics of biblical revelation and turning to the more speculative aspects of trinitarian theologizing, we might observe that, following Augustine, theologians have often suggested that the Spirit is the Bond of Love between the Father and the Son. If one takes this position, he *may* argue that because the Spirit is the Bond of Love in the Trinity itself, he is appropriately the One, in the economy of redemption, who effectually calls and illumines the sinner with true wisdom and so restores the bond of love between God and humankind.[22] But there is nothing in this trinitarian theorizing that would suggest that this eternal Bond of Love between the Father and the Son should be associated with the female—or, for that matter, the male—principle.

The same may be said of the argument from the fact that in the Apostles' Creed Jesus is said to be "conceived by the Holy Spirit." Of course, at the human level, females, not males, conceive. But obviously this language, similar to the common translation of Matthew 1:20, "that which is conceived in her is of the Holy Spirit," was never intended by the church to suggest that the Spirit be identified with the feminine principle. The church uses the language of conception when speaking of the Spirit's mysterious energizing of the Virgin, to avoid the suggestion that in the Incarnation the Spirit assumed the role of the Father of Jesus by impreg-

---

[22]Barth appears to argue thus in *Kirchliche Dogmatick*, I, 1, 504.

nating his mother. Jesus' Father is the first Person, not the third Person, of the Godhead. He is *begotten* of the Father, *conceived* by the Spirit, and *born* of the Virgin Mary. The virgin birth tells us not only that Jesus had no earthly father, but also that he had no heavenly mother.[23]

And so, no matter how one looks at it—whether from the data of comparative religions, the exegetical possibilities of the biblical text, or the erudite implications of trinitarian theologizing—the argument that identifies the Spirit with the female principle is without secure foundation. And even if one were not aware of its doubtful pedigree in Eastern non-Christian cults, one could sense that it is not a good argument in that it does not help us overcome what has been called the "bad masculine," that is, the traditional male distortions in our thinking about God as a masculine Deity. To suggest that the Trinity is a fellowship of two male Persons and one female Person who "proceeds" from them, would seem to ground the preeminence of the masculine in the very being of God himself. Then we would be back to the old argument that the man, at the creaturely level, is active and creative, the woman passive and receptive, because God himself is the Father who, from all eternity, actively begets the Son and with the Son spirates (breathes) the Spirit; whereas the Spirit is the One whose being is passively received from the Father and the Son. As the Spirit is *of* the Father in the work of the Godhead *ad intra*, so the woman is *of* (and *for*) the man in the work of the Godhead *ad extra*, that is, in creation.

This is really a very typical masculine argument.[24] While the church, reflecting on the biblical data, has conceived the mystery of the Godhead after the analogy of a personal fellowship, *this* argument conceives the Godhead after the analogy of a particular *form* of personal fellowship, namely, the family, and a *patriarchal* family at that. In this heavenly family, God the Father is the fountainhead of divinity, as the earthly father is the head of the human family.

[23]See K. Barth, *Kirchliche Dogmatik*, I, 1, 510.
[24]Observe its use by Myers in the quotation above, p. 44, note 16.

And in this heavenly family the Father begets a Son, as earthly fathers have begotten sons. Of course, there is also a Mother in this heavenly family, named last after the Father and the Son, and naturally so, because she derives her very being from them.

Such an interpretation of the doctrine of the Trinity, an interpretation reflected in the Bavarian fresco reproduced on page ii (and assumed in certain supposedly Christian psychological theories of marriage counseling), we can only reject out of hand for reasons already made clear. We therefore must conclude that the supposed solution to sexist theological language—or, we might better say, the traditionally sexist understanding of theological language—about God is not to be found in the assigning of the members of the Godhead to the male/female genders respectively. It is rather to be found in the affirmation of the orthodox view that God-in-himself, as a personal fellowship, transcends all distinctions of sex, yet condescends to compare himself to both sexes, likening himself to a Father whose pity knows no bounds (Ps. 103:13) and a Mother whose love can never fail (Isa. 66:13).[25]

---

[25]In Luke 15 there are three well-known parables: (1) the parable of the lost sheep (vv. 1–7); (2) the lost coin (vv. 8–10); and (3) the lost son (vv. 11–32). While the accent in all of them is on the joy occasioned by the finding of the lost (even the angels rejoice over one sinner who repents), it is commonly (and we believe rightly) assumed that God may be likened to the seeking shepherd (1), the searching woman (2), and the waiting father (3). The question is, may we go further than this? In view of the fact that Jesus elsewhere speaks of God as a Father, as in the last parable, and of himself as a Shepherd, as in the first parable, may we affirm that the parable about the father has to do with the first Person and the parable of the shepherd with the second Person of the Godhead? If so, then is it not plausible that the parable of the woman is not only representative of God generally, but of the Holy Spirit specifically, the One who effectually calls the sinner and so "finds" him, as the woman in the parable found the lost coin? While it would be too much to conclude that Jesus, in speaking these parables, or the early church, in preserving them, thought in terms so precisely trinitarian, yet we can see no objection to viewing them in this way. If God may be likened to a woman as well as to a man, to a mother as well as to a father, then may not the Holy Spirit, who is God, be likened specifically to a woman who is a housewife? This suggestion was first brought to my attention by Kay Lindskoog, whose perception can be discerned in other places in this study.

3. The Incarnation and the Historical Dimension

The conclusion that God is equally like man and woman is simply the correlate of the truth we have already espoused that men and women are equally like God, since he created humankind in his image as male and female. When one perceives the truth of these complementary affirmations, it becomes difficult to accept the position that there is some mysterious reason "in the nature of things" that requires that the Incarnation should take the form that it did. Whereas it has traditionally been assumed that both the nature of the second Person of the Godhead as "the eternal Son" and the nature of the male human being as the "image and glory of God" in whom the "discretion of reason predominates" required that the Incarnation should have taken the form of male humanity, this conclusion can hardly be sustained. And why? Because the assumptions on which it is based cannot be established. The trinitarian fellowship of the Godhead knows no male and female distinction, and the human fellowship of male and female knows no discrimination against the female as bearing the divine image to a lesser degree. Therefore, God's Incarnation in the form of male humanity is *theologically indifferent.*

We are not suggesting, however, that it was *historically* and *culturally* indifferent. Though God himself transcends all distinction between male and female, and though male and female on the human level are equally like God and, therefore, equally capable in themselves of mediating his self-revelation; it is not difficult, given the character of Jewish culture, to perceive why God chose to enter our world as a first-century Jew rather than a first-century Jewess. In the strongly patriarchal society of Israel, where the father was the head of the family and the son the heir of the family, it was only fitting that God should have disclosed himself primarily under the name of *Father* (Jer. 31:9; Mal. 1:6) and should have said to him who came in his name, "Thou art my *Son* (Matt. 3:17; Mark 1:11; Luke 3:22). Though we recognize that these trinitarian names of "Father" and "Son" are used analogically, and though we acknowledge that Jesus is not in eternity the "Son" of the

Father in the same literal sense that he became in time the "Son" of Mary, yet, given the condescension of God in revealing the mystery of his being to his ancient people in and through the name "Father," it is only reasonable that his final, personal self-disclosure in human history should have been in the form of a man who called God his Father and who was acknowledged to be his Son.

Thus we would counter the argument that since Jesus was the unique Son of God, he must have known what he was doing when he became incarnate as a *man*. Our reply is simply that he did indeed. And what exactly was he doing? He was entering into the stream of human life, and this human life had a history. He was crossing the line, coming from beyond time and place into *our* time and place, into *our* history; this is the meaning of the Incarnation. Therefore, he could not ignore the actualities of the historical situation.[26] What John Baillie has called the "scandal of particularity," that is, that God should have uniquely revealed himself in one particular man, a scandal that was heightened for the pagan Celsus by the thought that this man was not a Roman but a Jew, indeed, a crucified Jew, would have reached its apogee had this crucified Jew been a woman. We may indeed surmise, in such a case, that the incognito (to speak with Kierkegaard) of human personality, in which the divine Person was revealed, would scarcely have been penetrated even by the eye of the most discerning faith. While it may well be that revelation is what Kierkegaard called "indirect communication," if this communication were so indirect that it did not communicate, then revelation would no longer be revelation.

But all of this is simply to admit, in the last analysis, that there is no *ultimate* reason, either in the nature of the divine Creator or the human creature, but only in the nature of the historical situation, that both men and women should commit themselves to a *man* for their salvation. In faith the Christian, to be sure, acknowledges that Jesus, a Jew of the

[26]See Leonard Hodgson, who makes this point in his "Theological Objections [Answered] to the Ordination of Women," *Expository Times*, 77 (1965–1966):210–13.

first century, is Lord; but this does not imply that salvation is of the male as such. Salvation is of the *Lord*; this is the meaning of the fundamental confession that makes one a Christian.

ADDENDUM: A COMMENT ON GEORGE MACDONALD'S "THE WISE WOMAN, OR THE LOST PRINCESS: A DOUBLE STORY"[27]

Many who read what has just been said about the theological indifference of the male form of the Incarnation will no doubt say that they cannot imagine God's coming to us as Savior and Lord in the form of a woman. Perhaps their imaginations need conversion! This, according to C. S. Lewis, was what happened to him when he first read *Phantastes* by George MacDonald. "What it actually did to me," he says, "was to convert, even to baptize... my imagination."[28] George MacDonald was a nineteenth-century master of fantasy who wrote, as he said, not "for children, but for the childlike, whether of five, or fifty, or seventy-five." His writings not only delighted generations of children, but influenced Charles Williams, C. S. Lewis, J. R. R. Tolkien, and many others. The story which we have in mind, about a wise woman, is remarkable for the fact that it represents God as a female, though it is not clear whether she is Christ our Savior or the sanctifying Spirit.

After reading in the previous addendum, "The Holy Spirit as Female(?)," that the divine Wisdom revealed in Jesus our Lord is personified in the Old Testament as female, we might well conclude that our author intended to speak of the Savior in the figure of a wise woman. On the other hand, as the story unfolds, the saving work of the woman reminds one in many ways of what theologians describe as the work of sanctification, wrought by the Holy Spirit. It is the Spirit

[27]The text, first serialized under the title "A Double Story" in *Good Things* (1874), may be conveniently found in George MacDonald, *The Gifts of the Child Christ: Fairy Tales and Stories for the Childlike*, ed. Glenn Edward Sadler (Grand Rapids: Eerdmans, 1973), 1:199ff.

[28]Judging from his aversion to women priests, the conversion of Lewis' imagination was—like all conversions—semi-eschatological in nature!

of God who sheds abroad God's love in our hearts (Rom. 5:5)
and so mortifies the pride and self-love which almost destroyed the little princess, Rosamond, of whom MacDonald
tells us. But it would spoil the story were one to make the
question paramount, "Did the author have in mind the Son
or the Spirit?" As MacDonald himself once observed in an
essay entitled "The Fantastic Imagination," the reader of
one of his fairy tales should not ask,

> How am I to assure myself that I am not reading my
> own meaning into it but yours out of it? Why [he
> responds] should you be so assured? It may be better
> that you should read your meaning into it. That may
> be a higher operation of your intellect than the mere
> reading of mine out of it: your meaning may be
> superior to mine.[29]

MacDonald goes on to observe that a genuine work of art
means many things and does not need "THIS IS A HORSE"
written under it. His stories, he says, are written not so
much to *convey* a meaning as to *awake* a meaning. And
surely most of us, especially those who are males, need to
have the meaning of God our Redeemer appearing as a
woman *awakened* in us. And, again, who can better help us
here than a supreme master of that faculty in the human
spirit by which we delight to call up new forms for old
truths, the faculty which George MacDonald aptly called
"the fantastic imagination"? Therefore, let all serious students of theology lay aside their Greek and Hebrew exer-
cises, their tomes of dogmatic theology, long enough to read
MacDonald's story, "The Wise Woman," in order that they
themselves may become a little wiser.

4. The Male Apostolate and the Historical Dimension

a. Introduction

As the Incarnation in the form of male humanity can hardly
be understood apart from the actualities of the historical
situation, so it is also with the constitution of a male aposto-

[29]*Ibid.*, p. 25. Only very gifted and humble people can write out of
such security!

late. Even as he himself appeared as a man, our Lord also commissioned men to go and make disciples in his name. Though it is true that in Christ there is no male and female (Gal. 3:28), yet the apostles whom Christ commissioned had to preach in a world that knew male and female in terms of headship and submission, superiority and inferiority. While our Lord's intent, through the preaching of the apostles, was to redeem humankind and thus to create a new humanity in which the traditional divisions and antagonisms of the sexes would be reconciled, such redemption could not be accomplished simply by confrontation. We should not be surprised, then, that Jesus chose only men to herald the truth of the gospel in the Greco-Roman world of the first century.[30]

It would seem, in other words, that when it comes to the *original* apostolate, one should look upon its male character as having no more (and no less) theological significance than its Jewish character. Since the witness of the apostles was to *begin* in Jerusalem and Judea, since they came with a message "to the Jew *first*" and *then* "also to the Greek" (Acts 1:8; Rom. 1:16), is it to be wondered at that our Lord chose men who, like himself, were Jews? But if no one would reason that because Jesus and the original apostles were all Jews, therefore the Christian ministry should be Jewish to perpetuity, why reason from the fact that they were all men to the conclusion that it should be *male* to perpetuity?[31]

In response to this question, it has been argued that

[30]Those who reject the view that the male apostolate may be understood in terms of historical expediency argue that since women were accepted on an equal footing with men into the Christian church by baptism, it would be absurd to suppose that the Head of the Church limited the apostolate to men simply as a concession to the prejudices of the times. He would then have misled his church as to the true status of women. Thus Mascall observes that even Jesus' enemies never accused him of compromise or cowardice, and it ill becomes his followers in the 20th century to do so! ("Women and the Priesthood of the Church," p. 102). Such reasoning is unconvincing to the writer because it twists the terms of the argument so as to prejudice the case. "Expediency" is one thing, "compromise" and "cowardice" another.

[31]See Georgia Harkness, *Woman in Church and Society* (Nashville: Abingdon Press, 1971), p. 217. If one grants the validity of the Roman Catholic appeal to the "eternal feminine" at this juncture, then, indeed, the

the church was guided by his Spirit, after Jesus ascended, to admit Gentiles into membership on equal terms with Jews. Therefore, the New Testament does not warrant the exclusion of Gentiles from the ministry, there being no impediment, as is the case with women, to their admission. Furthermore, when one examines the qualifications for the office of elder or deacon given in the Pastorals, there is no distinction between Jew and Gentile implied; anyone can aspire to the office of the ministry who is an exemplary husband or father (I Tim. 3:1–3). But women, who are not husbands and fathers, for this very reason are not to assume the authority of the teaching office (I Tim. 2:12–14).

While this is a plausible conclusion in view of certain affirmations in the New Testament, it must also be remembered that in Christ there is neither male nor female, even as there is neither Jew nor Gentile. In other words, the same Spirit who inspired the church to eliminate all barriers to accepting Gentiles on the same footing with Jews, also inspired her to eliminate all barriers to accepting women on the same footing with men. Hence one would expect to find more in the New Testament bearing on this issue of women in the ministry than meets the eye at first glance. And this expectation is not disappointed. A close examination of the New Testament data shows that the Spirit guided the church not only to go beyond the Jewish constitution of the original apostolate, but, in a way, beyond its male constitution also. To say as much is not to deny that even as the original apostles were all men, so were those who shared the office of ministry under them. This the Pastorals plainly imply in spelling out the qualifications for the office of presbyter. Yet, on the other hand, the New Testament is not without evidence that points beyond this limitation, evidence the more remarkable when one considers the circumstances and times

---

parallelism between the Jewishness and the maleness of the original apostolate (which we are here arguing) cannot be sustained. Hence we will return to this question when dealing specifically with the Roman Catholic position on the ministerial priesthood. See below, pp. 88ff.

in which the Christian church was born. To this other evidence we shall now turn our attention.

b. Women as Witnesses to the Resurrection of Jesus

It is a commonplace of biblical scholarship that the resurrection is the central theme of the apostolic kerygma (Acts 2:22–34). The apostles testified to the fact that Jesus, who had been crucified, dead, and buried, had been raised from the dead. They had seen him (I Cor. 15:5f.), touched him (I John 1:1), and even eaten with him after his resurrection (Acts 10:41). In his name, therefore, they proclaimed salvation.

In view of the great importance of this apostolic witness to the resurrection, it can hardly be wholly inconsequential that the risen Lord appeared first to women. The fact that they were first at the tomb could, indeed, be attributed to the accidents of history. These women were only doing their womanly duty when they came early to the sepulchre to anoint the body of the deceased. Hence they happened to discover the empty tomb. But that the risen Lord appeared first to these women (Matt. 28:9; John 20:11ff.) and even commissioned them to tell his brethren (Matt. 28:10) cannot be construed as mere coincidence. It was the result of a deliberate choice on his part. Thus these women disciples became the initial witnesses to the event which is the basis of all Christian preaching. Of course, the male disciples did not believe their witness; they regarded what these women had to say as so many idle tales (Luke 24:11).[32] Even Paul does not mention their witness in his first letter to the Corinthians, beginning rather with Peter and the twelve (I Cor. 15:5). But it is true, for all that, that the women closest to our Lord were witnesses—in fact, the

---

[32]Renan (following Celsus), in his *Vie de Jesus*, singles out Mary Magdalene as the unstable female who perpetrated the idle tale of the resurrection on the world. As a typical male chauvinist he comments disparagingly, "The passion of an hallucinated woman gave the world a risen God!" (as quoted by Philip Schaff, *History of the Christian Church* [Grand Rapids: Eerdmans, 1955], 1:179, note 1).

first witnesses—to the central truth of the Christian kerygma: "this Jesus did God raise up" (Acts 2:32).[33]

One cannot say that the original apostolic preaching was based on the witness of the women, for the apostles themselves all had direct and indubitable encounters with the risen Lord, including Paul, the great apostle to the Gentiles (Acts 9:1–6; I Cor. 15:8). But one can say that women shared with men in that witness in the beginning in a way that has not been ordinarily allowed to them throughout the following centuries of Christian proclamation. Since this early sharing was due to an act of the risen Lord himself, it should not be ignored as the church today seeks the mind of Christ in the matter of admitting women to the office of ministry on the same terms as men.[34]

c. Women Present at Pentecost and Endowed with the Prophetic Gift

Not only were women co-witnesses with men of the resurrection, but they also shared with them in the Pentecostal effusion of the Spirit, though in this latter instance the evidence is perhaps not so striking. Women were not given a priority; in fact, it was to the eleven, all of whom were men, that the command was given to wait in Jerusalem for the promise of the Spirit's baptism (Acts 1:4–5).[35] But women are mentioned, including Mary, Jesus' mother, as among those gathered with the apostles in prayerful expectation when the Spirit came. The statement in Acts is that cloven

[33]Speaking of women as the first witnesses to the resurrection, the following datum is interesting. The Johannine tradition (John 4:39) locates the witness of the Samaritan woman ("many believed on him because of the word of the woman") earlier in the sequence of events in Jesus' life than the synoptic report of Peter's confession at Caesarea Philippi (Mark 8:27–30 par.). One can easily perceive this interesting fact by consulting any standard harmony of the four Gospels.

[34]It is true that in the Gospels all the express invitations to follow him are addressed by Jesus to men. Yet surely the many women who followed him must have done so with his blessing and approval.

[35]However one may relate John 20:22—"he breathed on them and said to them, Receive the Holy Spirit"—to the account in Acts of the coming of the Spirit, here too, only men were involved.

tongues as of fire rested on each of them, and they were all filled with the Holy Spirit and began to speak in other tongues as the Spirit gave them utterance (Acts 2:3–4). There is no sufficient reason for limiting this statement, as has been traditionally done, to men, since Peter himself explains what happened by quoting the prophet Joel: "I will pour out my Spirit upon all flesh and your sons *and your daughters* shall prophesy" (Acts 2:17).

While it is true that Peter is the primary spokesman for the group, we should not conclude that only men spoke on this occasion. Luke does not describe the speakers beyond the detail that they were Galileans (Acts 2:7), but in his Gospel he makes specific reference to women present at Jesus' crucifixion and burial "who had followed him from Galilee" (Luke 23:49, 55). It would seem reasonable, therefore, to suppose that some of these very women may have received the Spirit of prophecy and exercised the gift from the inception of the Christian church. In other words, when we read that the church is built upon the foundation of the apostles and prophets (Eph. 2:20), while we know that the former were all men, we also know that the latter were not all men: there were prophetesses as well as prophets in the apostolic church, and some of them may have been active from its inception.

To affirm that there were women prophets in the New Testament church, women who spoke "as the Spirit gave them utterance," would not suggest an unheard-of phenomenon, something utterly unthinkable in the light of the church's Jewish antecedents. There were occasional prophetesses even in the Old Testament. Miriam, the sister of Moses, is called a prophetess (Exod. 15:20), as well as Deborah, who ruled over Israel in the days of the judges (Judges 4:4); Huldah the prophetess was consulted by the king, no less, at the time Hilkiah the high priest "found the book of the law in the house of the Lord" (II Kings 22:8, 14ff.). Even the false prophetesses against whom Ezekiel indicts an awful judgment (Ezek. 13:17–23) by their very existence imply that there were true prophetesses in Israel. Only the genuine can be counterfeited.[36] In the New Testament, the devout Jewess Anna, who bore witness to the infant Jesus at the time of his presentation in the temple (Luke 2:36), is called a prophetess. Such an act on her part was in keeping with the meaning of the word "prophet" as it came to be used in the New Testament church. The New Testament prophet was one who proclaimed a divinely inspired message; hence the prophets were inspired teachers of the early church (Acts 19:6; 21:9; Rom. 12:6; I Cor. 12:10; 13:2, 8; 14:6; I Thess. 5:20).

On the other hand, knowing as we do the dominant place of the male in first-century Jewish society, especially in the synagogue, it can hardly be doubted that the use of the gift of prophecy by women in the early church was considered exceptional and in some sense problematical. In the Corinthian congregation, for example, there were women who received and used the gift (I Cor. 11:5); yet we have an enigmatical injunction to silence imposed upon the women of this very congregation (I Cor. 14:33ff.). Some scholars have felt this same ambivalence in the mention of Philip's four virgin daughters who prophesied (Acts 21:9). The way in which this notice is inserted by the author, without any immediate connection with the historical narrative, seems to indicate that it was considered by Luke an altogether remarkable circumstance that should be brought to his readers' attention.[37] The fact that he says they prophesied, but not that they were prophets, may reflect a reticence which made it easier to speak of their function than to give them, as women, the title which such a function implied.

The ambivalence that one feels in the New Testament data concerning women who exercised the prophetic gift has been resolved by some interpreters by granting such

---

[36]These counterfeit prophetesses were probably more like sorcerers than prophets. A New Testament parallel would be the seducer Jezebel "who calls herself a prophetess" (Rev. 2:20).

[37]The more remarkable, of course, in that the women were all virgins. Some have speculated that Luke may have mentioned them because they were a source of his information in preparing his history.

women a very limited ministry. Calvin, for example, commenting on Philip's daughters, observes:

> It is uncertain how these maids did execute the office of prophesying, save that the Spirit of God did so guide and govern them, that he did not overthrow the order which he himself set down. And forasmuch as he does not suffer women to bear any public office in the Church, it is to be thought that they did prophesy at home, or in some private place, without the common assembly.[38]

While this conclusion is perhaps too neat, it seems obvious that as the church developed, the subordinate role of women in society overcame the teaching authority implicit in the prophetic gift. In the Pastorals, accordingly, we find an express statement barring all women from the teaching office because they are women (I Tim. 2:12). There is no counterbalancing thought that in exceptional cases they might be ordained, like men, as inspired teachers of the church. As time went on, the dying out of pneumatic manifestations in the mainstream of the church's congregational life no doubt aided and abetted this curtailing of the woman's function as a teacher in the church. The final result was the medieval convent as the only "proper place" for a woman called to serve Christ in an official way.

Such a curtailing of the woman's role, however, cannot—at least it should not—neutralize the plain testimony of the New Testament to the truth that women not only saw the risen Christ and bore witness to him but also shared with men in the outpouring of his Spirit, and so were qualified even as the male disciples to be his witnesses (Acts 1:8). *In other words, the qualifications that men brought to the office of ministry in the New Testament, women also brought.* Over against the fact, so frequently stressed, that only men were admitted, in a formal way, to the office of ministry in the New Testament church, this truth needs to be underscored. Only in the light of this truth will we see

[38]*Commentary on Acts* (Grand Rapids: Eerdmans, 1966).

the total picture of the place of women in the church and appreciate the manner in which the New Testament sources, while reflecting the historical situation in which they were produced, yet point beyond their times to a more adequate model of fellowship in Christ, a fellowship which imposes no barriers between the feminine half of the church and the office of ministry.[39]

d. Women in the Pauline Congregations

There are, to be sure, passages in the Pauline letters which point in another direction from that which we are advocating. These passages (to which we have alluded from time to time) do not concern the office of ministry directly, yet they indirectly apply to the question before us, since those who are entrusted with the privilege of the ministerial office are thereby vested with the authority which such a privilege entails. There are several passing references to this authority in the New Testament. Paul, for example, exhorts the Thessalonians to recognize those "who labor among you and are over you" (I Thess. 5:12); twice the author of Hebrews admonishes his/her[40] readers to "obey those who have the rule over you and submit to them" (13:17, 24); the First Epistle to Timothy alludes to "elders who rule well" (5:17); and First Peter instructs elders to exercise the oversight of the flock with exemplary restraint and humility (5:1–3). Since the office of ministry implies a distinction between those who rule and those who are ruled, those who have the oversight

[39]In Pentecostal churches women share with men in the ministerial office. Appeal is made to the outpouring of the Spirit in the book of Acts on "sons and daughters" alike. Such women tend to harmonize their equality in Christ in this respect with the teaching of the New Testament about subordination of women to men by limiting this subordination to the husband/wife relationship. The author recalls hearing a woman Pentecostal preacher on a Sunday morning in a ghost town in Colorado. She had followed her husband, who was a prospector and miner, to a place where churches had been boarded up when the mines and mills had closed. Having reopened one of these antiquated edifices, she sought, as a submissive wife, to exercise her calling as a minister of the gospel and teacher of a Christian congregation in the place where her husband chose to labor.

[40]Is not the ultimate problem with the hypothesis that Priscilla wrote Hebrews that it violates the canon which says that a woman could not write Scripture?

and those who are subject to such oversight, obviously one cannot affirm the woman's right to such an office without coming to terms with the traditional notion of sexual hierarchy whereby she is subordinate to the man. If God created the woman to be in submission to the man, so that "it is not possible in the female sex to signify eminence of degree" (St. Thomas), then she can hardly exercise the authority over the man which ordination would give her in the life and affairs of the Christian congregation.

Passages, therefore, especially in the Pauline letters, which seem to imply the woman's subordination to the man, are invariably cited when women's ordination is advocated. We are reminded that Paul regarded the man as the "head of the woman" (I Cor. 11:3); that he enjoined silence upon women in church (I Cor. 14:33b–35); and that women are to learn in quietness, with all subjection, not being permitted to teach nor to have dominion over the man (I Tim. 2:11).

The response of those who advocate the woman's right to the ministerial office varies greatly. Some dismiss Paul out of hand as a hopeless misogynist. Others seek to reinterpret the so-called problem passages in his epistles so as to give them a meaning amenable to the practice of sexual parity in the church of Christ. While the former position seems to us wholly unwarranted in the light of Paul's teaching as a whole, the latter position is not without its difficulties as well. Efforts to construe Paul's remarks about the man/woman relationship as mere adaptation to his culture, qualification of the silence which he enjoins upon women in church as simply placing a restraint upon the obstreperous questions and garrulous ignorance of certain women in Corinth, efforts to show that the proscription of the woman's teaching does not mean she cannot teach but only that she cannot teach "in an official capacity" or that she should not do so in an autocratic and unbending way, are hardly convincing.

To be sure, there are mediating positions between these extremes; yet, when all is said and done, it seems to us that in the passages mentioned above, Paul does, in a marked way, delimit the woman's place in the worshiping

congregation. We prefer, therefore, to recognize this strand
of Paul's thought for what it is, a statement of sexual hierarchy. Yet it is by no means the rigorous form of sexual hierarchy found in the Old Testament, for he was profoundly convinced that in Christ there can be neither Jew nor Greek,
bond nor free, male nor female (Gal. 3:28). The implications
of the oneness of the family of God whereby we are all his
children through faith in Christ Jesus (Gal. 3:26), he pressed
most rigorously in the matter of Jew and Greek. In fact, he
withstood Peter to his face in Antioch for not living out, in
this regard, the implications of the Christian faith in an
ethnically mixed congregation (Gal. 2:11f.). He is more restrained when it comes to the master/slave relationship,
even admonishing slaves to obey their masters, as he ad-
monished wives to submit to their husbands (Eph. 5:22–6:6;
Col. 3:22; Titus 2:9). Yet even here, he perceived things in a
new light, as can be seen from his letter to Philemon, where
he instructs a slaveholder not only to forgive a runaway
slave his debt, but—unheard-of thought—to receive him back
as a brother (v. 16). So also when it comes to male and female,
though Paul did not press all the implications rigorously, he
surely did grasp the essential truth that the revelation of God
in Christ radically affects the man/woman relationship. We
know this not only from the magnificent affirmation that in
Christ there is no male and female, but also from the way in
which he related to women as a Christian apostle. Read in
this light, one can appreciate anew those hints in his letters
that women enjoyed a larger privilege in the churches where
he labored than might be supposed in the light of subsequent
centuries of Christian tradition. When he wrote to the Philippians, for example, publicly exhorting "Euodia and Syntyche
to be of the same mind in the Lord" (4:2), there was no suggestion that the prominence in the congregation which this
public exhortation implied should be curtailed because they
were women. In fact, he reinforced his appeal to them by reminding them that they had been his colleagues, working
side by side with him. These were women who "labored with
me in the gospel" (4:3), which, as W. Derek Thomas sug-

gests, surely means more than serving meals, sewing aprons, and sending supplies to the mission field:

> Paul uses a strong word... συνήθλησαν (Phil. 4:3). The verb ἀθλέω meant "to contend," as the athlete strained every muscle to achieve victory in the games. So, with equal dedication these women had contended with all zeal for the victory of the Gospel at Philippi. The Apostle had already used the same word in the first chapter, ". . . with one mind striving side by side for the faith of the Gospel. . . ," where the word suggests the side-by-side contending for the defense of the Gospel in Christian witness and apologetic.
>
> The Apostle would scarcely have used this strong word if they had merely "assisted him with material help" and hospitality, while remaining in the background. The word συνήθλησαν suggests a more active participation in the work of Paul, probably even a vocal declaration of the faith. How far this is true is admittedly a matter of conjecture; what can be said with certainty, however, is that they had contended with the Apostle in the cause of the Gospel and had gained a position of such influence as to make their present conflict a risk to the wellbeing of the church.[41]

Hence there is good reason to suppose that Paul not only knew the place women had enjoyed in those great revelatory events—Easter and Pentecost—on which the church was founded, but that he also acted in the light of what he knew by acknowledging the place of certain dedicated women in the important task of founding the church and establishing its ongoing witness. Among such women were the affluent businesswoman Lydia, his first convert in Europe, who opened her home to the Philippian congrega-

---

[41]"The Place of Women in the Church at Philippi," *Expository Times*, 83 (1972):117–20. In this perceptive article the author also cites Polycarp's Philippian letter, in which the martyr bishop of Smyrna (died, Feb., A. D. 155) admonishes wives to love their husbands without mention of wifely fear (see "Polycarp to the Philippians," *The Apostolic Fathers*, 1 [1949]:301).

tion (Acts 16:14–15); Priscilla of Rome, whom he calls his fellow worker (συνεργός) in the gospel (Rom. 16:3); and Phoebe, whom he commends as a servant of the church in Cenchreae and a helper (προστάτις) of many, whose business in Rome warranted the support of all the saints (Rom. 16:1–2).[42]

ADDENDUM: WOMEN—APOSTLES AND DEACONS IN THE NEW TESTAMENT?

Though not persuaded of the traditional argument against admitting women to the ministry drawn from the fact that Jesus appointed only men as apostles, we have not contested that fact as such, nor that their immediate successors in the ministerial office (as the Pastorals show) were men. We must comment, however, on details of the New Testament text which can be and have been construed otherwise by those favoring the admission of women to this office.

In Romans 16:7 Paul sends greetings to two friends in the following words: "Greet Andronicus and Junias/Junia, my kindred and fellow prisoners, who are of note among the apostles." Since the original manuscripts are without accents, the form of the second name here used may be construed either as masculine (Ἰουνιᾶν) or as feminine (Ἰουνίαν) and hence translated either as "Junias" or "Junia."[43] The added phrase, οἵτινές εἰσιν ἐπίσημοι ἐν τοῖς ἀποστόλοις, is also susceptible of more than one meaning. It may mean, "who are well-known among the apostles"; or it may mean, "who are among those called apostles and notably so." The former interpretation suggests an intimacy among a rather closely-knit group called "the apostles," an intimacy which Paul, at least, did not seem to know (Gal. 1–2). Hence some prefer the latter interpretation, which would include two

[42]Though προστάτις means etymologically "a woman who stands before (over) others," it is not likely that Phoebe is here described as a woman "ruler of many people." Rather, the meaning is more likely that she is one who cares for the affairs of many by aiding them with her resources, i.e., as a "patron," "sponsor," or "protector."

[43]The Fragment p46 reads Ἰουλιαν; but since this may be taken as a masculine (Julius) or a feminine (Julia), this alternate reading has no bearing on the question of the sex of the person named.

persons named Andronicus and Junias/Junia in the company of the apostles. Were one to give the text such a rendering, then the term "apostles" must be understood loosely of all those sent forth in Christ's name, since no one named Andronicus or Junias belonged to the group of apostles immediately chosen by Christ. Even given this looser sense, one wonders if a woman would have been called an "apostle" in her own right in New Testament times. Thus most translators favor the masculine rendering, "Junias," understanding Paul to be speaking of two men, Andronicus and Junias, who were associated in Christian ministry.

It is possible, however, to suppose that this greeting is sent to a man and his wife, who might be compared in this respect to Priscilla and Aquila, whom Paul calls his "fellow workers" (συνεϱγούς) in Christ (Rom. 16:3). Since the latter couple were called "fellow workers" with one who was himself an apostle, might not the former couple, as man and wife, be deemed worthy of the name "apostles" in the general sense of "messengers of Christ"? At least so it would seem, especially if they were intimately associated with certain of the original apostles. Hence the plausibility of the suggestion that Paul is greeting a man and a woman in this passage, calling them "apostles" in a general sense.

As for those who succeeded the apostles, specifically those appointed by them to the office of elder/bishop (synonymous terms in the New Testament), there is a general consensus, as we have observed, that no women were admitted to this privilege. However, it is commonly assumed that in the New Testament there was a lesser office of deacon and that women shared its responsibilities with men; that is, they functioned as deaconesses. It has traditionally been assumed that the appointing of "the seven" in Acts 6 marks the inception of this office. Such an assumption, however, is historically doubtful for the following reasons: the word "deacon" (διάϰονος, servant) does not occur in Acts 6; Philip, one of the "seven," is expressly called an evangelist (Acts 21:8); and when Paul, with Barnabas, carried relief to the poor saints in Jerusalem, it was given not to the "deacons" but to the elders (Acts 11:30).

The first clear mention of deacons is found in the salutation of Paul's letter to the Philippians. Yet here we have no more than the word itself used as a designation of those who render some particular service within the congregation. It is only at a later time (I Tim. 3:8–13) that we have the qualifications of deacons set forth. By this time it appears that a distinct office is in view, though nothing is said in the text about the task of those who are admitted to it. Hence one can only presume that deacons rendered various services in the local fellowship on the basis of their individual gifts.

In the midst of the passage in I Timothy, which spells out the qualifications of those who aspire to become deacons, there is a sentence (unexpectedly) admonishing women: "Women likewise must be grave, not slanderers, temperate, faithful in all things" (I Tim. 3:11). Since this verse admonishing women is preceded and followed by the qualifications for the office of deacon, one cannot escape the impression that the admonition must have something to do with the diaconate. But just what is not easy to determine. Some have construed the verse as a reference to deaconesses, because of the context, even though the word "deaconess" does not occur in the text. Others have suggested that the reference is to women who are *wives* of deacons, an interpretation which seems quite plausible in this context. However, it may be that by the time the Pastorals were written, not only wives but also certain other women assisted deacons in a way that anticipated the office of deaconess as it subsequently developed in the church.

As for the task of one who functions in the diaconate, it is only in the sub-apostolic age that the deacon emerges as the right hand of the bishop, assisting him in the worship service and distributing the gifts consecrated in worship to the poor and needy of the congregation. The first mention of women in this role is in the "Letter" of Pliny to Trajan (A.D. 109). Such serving women ("deaconesses," *ministrae*), especially in the Eastern usage, seem to have been the successors, not of the women mentioned in I Timothy 3:11, but of the "widows" who are prominently mentioned first in Acts

6:1 and 9:39–41 and later in I Timothy 5. These widows were the elderly women of the congregation who needed economic help and social support because of their situation. By the time the Pastorals were written, they constituted a special class in the church, leading, it may be, the feminine part of the congregation as models of Christian devotion and piety (I Tim. 5:3–16). Presumably they assumed various tasks among the women, visiting and instructing them (Titus 2:3–4) and rendering those services which might seem inappropriate to a male deacon. When Pliny wrote to the emperor, such women servants appear to have been officers with proper and specific duties such as assisting women converts in baptism and the like.

The office of deaconess, then, when it becomes a clearly developed one, reflects a concept of woman and her place in the church that is consonant with the received role of women in the society of the day. In this restricted sense, women have been ordained (some authorities use the word "blessed") as deaconesses down to the present day in the Greek Orthodox Church. In the mainstream of Western (Roman) Christianity, however, the office did not survive.[44] Its demise has been attributed to the decline of adult immersion, a rite in which propriety urged that women assist women—since immersion was in the nude; also to the reaction against the prominent ministry of women in certain heretical sects; and to the rise of female religious orders which assimilated and redirected the women's former deaconal functions.

Because service in general and the ministering of charitable aid to the members of her own sex in particular are activities considered proper to a woman, few Protestant theologians have felt any difficulty in affirming that deaconesses, such as those mentioned in the early second

---

[44]Canon 19 of the Nicene Council, A.D. 325, uses the word "deaconess," as do the third-century *Apostolic Constitutions* and the *Didascalia.* Also the Pontificals of Egbert, Archbishop of York, A.D. 732–766, and the Leafric Missal of the Bishop of Exeter, A.D. 1050–1072. Whether or not women were inducted into this office by "ordination," properly speaking, is a question on which there is no consensus among historians.

century by Pliny, served in the church from the age of the apostles. Having thus read the office back into the New Testament, they have identified Phoebe of Cenchreae as the first "deaconess" to be mentioned by name (Rom. 16:1). Male translators have sometimes fortified this conclusion by translating διάκονον in this passage by the technical term "deaconess," rather than by the general term "servant." Given such a translation, the apostle is made to say, "I commend to you our sister Phoebe, a 'deaconess' in the church in Cenchreae." Thus this woman, who delivered Paul's letter to the Romans with a cover letter from the apostle commending her to the church as worthy of whatever assistance she might need in carrying out her business (Rom. 16:2), is thought of as a Dorcas, who used her hands to sew coats and garments (Acts 9:39); or as one of those women, reverent in demeanor, who trained the young women to love their husbands and children, and to be sober-minded, chaste workers at home, in subjection to their husbands (Titus 2:4–5). But, as we have seen, there is reason to believe that Phoebe, and certain other women in the New Testament church, had roles considerably more significant than what is usually conveyed by the word "deaconess," roles which some who extol the office of deaconess would not deem proper for a woman in the church today nor even possible in the first century.[45]

C. CONCERNING THE VATICAN DECREE: "INTER INSIGNIORES"

1. Introduction

As laypersons, Catholic and Protestant women have functioned as administrators, preachers, and writers whose

---

[45]For a contemporary Roman Catholic statement, see Fr. Jean Danielou, S.J., *The Ministry of Women in the Early Church* (London and New York: Faith Press, 1961). Danielou recognizes that Phoebe was not a "deaconess," but approves this and similar roles for women in the church today based on the tradition that deaconesses and widows have been assigned special tasks in the church from very early times.

influence in the church has surpassed that of many in the ranks of the ordained clergy. However, such ministry has generally been under the shadow of men to whom the authority of the ministerial office belongs. In 1922, for example, the all-male General Assembly of the Presbyterian Church voted to merge the Women's Board of Foreign Missions with the Board of Foreign Missions. The purpose of the merger was not that women might share leadership with men in the multi-million dollar, worldwide mission program of the church (women were not even consulted), but rather that men might secure the leadership of this program to themselves exclusively.

Although many Protestant denominations have progressed far beyond such overt discrimination, the place of women in the Roman Catholic hierarchy remains virtually unchanged. Barbara Ward, prominent British economist and recognized expert on world poverty, had to sit in silence at Vatican II while a man read her address. Though a Catholic woman be a theologian and college president, she must defer to an altarboy when a pope requires an acolyte at Mass.

While some Catholics have said that women's exclusion from the priesthood is a cultural, not a theological, issue, those theologians who speak for the church have said nothing of the sort. Karl Rahner, for example, though circumspect, is very traditional in his pronouncements on the subject. In his essay, "The Position of Women in the New Situation in Which the Church Finds Herself," he does make the following points: the church needs to take into account the rising new class of professional women; women must have a voice in their own tasks; and there is much, in any case, for women to do in the church today. Yet he safeguards all this by saying that for the present one need not even discuss the woman's admission to holy orders or her place in the hierarchy. (It is, to be sure, a "rustling in the mulberry trees" that he should have so much as mentioned such an undiscussable subject.) He also states that the new, innovative efforts of women in the church are, of course, subject to the magisterium and oversight of the church. Of course! Little wonder that at the end of the essay he admits that he has not said much—surely not an overstatement.[46]

Rahner's essay was written in 1971. The magisterium has since spoken; in fact, it has even discussed at some length the possibility of women's ordination to the priesthood. This discussion is found in the Declaration, "Inter Insigniores," issued by the Congregation for the Doctrine of the Faith concerning the admission of women to the ministerial priesthood.[47] Because this "Declaration" has been reiterated unqualifiedly by Pope John Paul II, the successor of Paul VI (during whose reign it was promulgated), and because so many Roman Catholics had hoped that he would do otherwise, especially American nuns in the Leadership Conference of Women Religious, we have thought it appropriate to conclude our analysis of the traditional argument for a male order of Christian ministry by a review of and response to this document.

We will, in a way, repeat ourselves, for in discussing the nature of women, of the office of ministry, and of the God who calls those that minister in his name, we have already had occasion to refer to the traditional Roman Catholic perspective. We have, however, simply commented on facets of that perspective; we have not dealt with it in any depth. "Inter Insigniores" calls for such in-depth treatment because it is the most precise, and some would say, profound, argument *contra* the ordination of women ever made by the Magisterium of the Roman Catholic Church. And it has the endorsement of major spokesmen for the Eastern Orthodox tradition.

The immediate occasion for the issuance of the Declaration was undoubtedly the decision of the Episcopal Church in America, a member of the worldwide Anglican

[46]This essay is translated in his *Theological Investigations* (New York: Herder and Herder, 1971), vol. 8, part 2, pp. 75–93.
[47]For the full text see *L'Osservatore Romano*, February 3, 1977, pp. 6–8. It was approved by the Pope on Oct. 15, 1976, the feast of St. Theresa of Avila, and signed by the Prefect of the Sacred Congregation, Franjo Cardinal Seper. An American commentary has been issued with the text by the United States Catholic Conference, Washington, D.C.

Communion, to ordain women to the priesthood.[48] This decision, and the growing consensus among Anglicans in the mother church of Britain favoring such action, provoked a sharp reaction among both Eastern Orthodox and Roman Catholics. While the Ecumenical Patriarch made no personal response to the Archbishop of Canterbury's letter advising him of the situation in the Anglican Communion, Eastern Orthodox theologians, as a whole, denounced the decision of the American Episcopalians with an unrestrained vehemence. Kallistos Ware, a member of the Monastic Brotherhood of St. John the Theologian, Spalding Lecturer in Eastern Orthodox Studies at the University of Oxford, fellow of Pembroke College, and secretary of the Anglican-Orthodox Joint Doctrinal Commission, observed,

> To an Orthodox Christian it seems not so much ironic as tragic that, at the very moment when Christians everywhere are praying for unity, we should see a new chasm opening up to divide us. And in Orthodox eyes, at any rate, it is a chasm of horrifying dimensions. "The ordination of women to priesthood," writes Fr. Alexander Schmemann, "is tantamount for us to a radical and irreparable mutilation of the entire faith, the rejection of the whole Scripture, and, needless to say, the end of all 'dialogues'"; and he goes on to speak about "the threat of an irreversible and irreparable act which, if it becomes reality, will produce a new, and this time, I am convinced, final division among Christians." According to another Orthodox spokesman, Fr. Thomas Hopko, the acceptance of women priests involves "a fundamental and radical rejection of the very substance of the biblical and Christian understanding of God and creation.... The decisions taken by the Episcopal

---

[48]This decision was reached (by a small majority) when the General Convention of the Episcopal Church of the United States of America authorized the ordination of women to the priesthood and their consecration to the episcopate in September, 1976. This was one of many such actions by ecclesiastical bodies going back to the decision of the Lutheran Church of Sweden to admit women to the pastoral office in 1958.

Church in America at its General Convention in
Minneapolis ... can only be considered by an Orthodox Christian as disastrous." These are strong
words. Yet Fr. Schmemann and Fr. Hopko are both of
them priests with a long pastoral experience in the
West, who have within their own communion the
reputation of being, in the best sense, progressive and
open-minded.[49]

As for the Roman Catholics, while their response was
less vehement, it was no less firm. Pope Paul VI made two
restrained but definite replies to the Anglican Archbishop in
which he lamented the decision of the American Episcopal
Communion to admit women to the ordained priesthood as
constituting a very "grave and new obstacle" on the path to
reconciliation, a path along which he had ardently hoped the
Holy Spirit would lead the Anglicans and Roman Catholics
in a like obedience to God's will.

2. A Summary of the Argument

As we turn to the argument in the "Inter Insigniores," it will
be recalled that in our previous discussion, we concluded
that, so far as the ordination of women is concerned, ultimately it makes no difference whether one opts for the
Roman Catholic or the Protestant concept of ministry. We
do not deny that in this matter there is a real and substantial
difference at the conceptual level between Catholics and
Protestants. (To the former, the ministerial office is a sacrament; to the latter, it is a service to the divine word as proclaimed in sermon and sacrament.) Nor do we deny that our
Roman Catholic friends regard this difference as having a
crucial bearing on the question, "Should women be ordained
to the priesthood?" On this latter point, however, we must dis-

[49]"Man, Woman, and the Priesthood of Christ," in Peter Moore,
ed., *Man, Woman, and Priesthood* (London: S.P.C.K., 1978), p. 69. Some of
the reasons for such strong statements we hope to illumine, for the Protestant reader, in the ensuing pages.

agree with them. We believe that the significant theological difference between the Catholic and Protestant understanding of the ministerial office does not justify the frequent claim which Catholic theologians make that women may serve as Protestant ministers but not as Catholic priests. While it is true, as Catholics often affirm, that "Protestants do not face the problem of women in the priesthood because they have dispensed with the priesthood altogether," it does not follow that because Catholics have affirmed the priesthood, they must deny women access to the priestly office.

In order to show how we come to such a conclusion, we need to examine the argument of the Vatican Declaration, particularly as it turns on the supposed difference between the universal priesthood of all believers and the individual priesthood of ministerial order. This difference is most sharply focused in—though not limited to—the priest as a celebrant of the Eucharist. The perspective of history helps one perceive why this is so. Early in the history of the church the Eucharist came to be understood not only as a communal meal but also as a sacramental reenactment of the atoning death of our Lord.[50] By the same token the presiding presbyter (πρεσβύτερος) at the Eucharistic meal came increasingly to be identified with Christ, the true Priest who made the original offering. This development, in turn, led to the view that the one who presides at the Eucharistic sacrifice is himself a priest (*sacerdos*) whose ministry in this central act of worship is a sacerdotal, that is, priestly, act. Of course the priest, when he so acts, does not act in his own name, i.e., *in persona propria*. Rather, he acts in the name of the whole congregation of God's people. As St. Thomas Aquinas teaches, "in the prayers of the Mass, the priest speaks *in persona Ecclesiae*, occupying the place of the

[50]The Protestant Reformers viewed this development as a departure from the teaching of the New Testament, while Roman Catholic apologists viewed it as a working out of what is implicit in the New Testament. Though our commitment is Protestant, we grant the Catholic position at this juncture for the sake of the argument.

church."[51] To this extent the doctrine of the universal priesthood of all believers bears on the meaning of the priestly office of ministry.

But for the Roman Catholic, as for the Eastern Orthodox, this priesthood of *sanctity*, as it is sometimes called, whereby all Christians, clergy and laity alike, are a royal priesthood, set apart to God's service (I Pet. 2:9), must not be confused (as it too often is in Protestant thought) with the ministerial priesthood of *order*. As for the former, universal priesthood, men and women alike participate in it, for they are equally created in the image of God, equally recreated in baptism (the "washing of regeneration," Titus 3:5) and equally endowed with the Spirit in confirmation (the "renewal of the Holy Spirit," again Titus 3:5). Were the celebrant of the Mass simply speaking *in persona Ecclesiae*, then surely women could so function. Indeed, there might be a special propriety in their presence at the altar, since the church, viewed as a whole, is female, the bride of Christ.

Why, then, is the ministerial priesthood not open to women? Because it is rendered not only *in persona Ecclesiae*, but also *in persona Christi*, who, as the Head of the Church, which is his body, is the one, true and only High Priest. And this latter consideration is basic to our discussion. The fact that the celebrating priest represents Christ gives the priesthood of order its primary meaning. As Pius XII affirmed in the Encyclical *Mediator Dei*, "The priest takes the people's place only because he plays the part of our Lord Jesus Christ, since Jesus is the Head of all his members and offers himself for them. . . ."[52] Hence the Vatican Declaration on the Order of Priesthood observes,

> However, it will perhaps be further objected that the priest, especially when he presides at the

[51]*Summa Theologica*, IIIa, q. 81, a. 7, *ad* 3 um, as cited by Monsignor A. G. Martimort, "The Value of the Theological Formula 'In persona Christi,'" in *The Order of Priesthood, Nine Commentaries on the Vatican Decree Inter Insigniores*, an OSV Source Book, Our Sunday Visitor, 1978, pp. 85f., hereafter cited as *The Order of Priesthood*.

[52]As quoted by Martimort, *ibid.*, p. 85.

liturgical and sacramental functions, equally represents the Church: he acts in her name with "the in-
tention of doing what she does." In this sense, the
theologians of the Middle Ages said that the minister
also acts *in persona Ecclesiae*, that is to say, in the
name of the whole Church and in order to represent
her. And in fact, leaving aside the question of the
participation of the faithful in a liturgical action, it is
in the name of the whole Church that the action is
celebrated by the priest: he prays in the name of all,
and in the Mass he offers the sacrifice of the whole
Church. In the new Passover, the Church, under
visible signs, immolates Christ through the mystery
of the priest. And so, it is asserted, since the priest
also represents the Church, would it not be possible
to think that this representation could be carried out
by a woman, according to the symbolism [the church
is the bride of Christ] already explained?

It is true that the priest represents the Church,
which is the Body of Christ. But if he does so, it is
precisely because he first represents Christ himself,
who is the Head and Shepherd of the Church. The
Second Vatican Council used this phrase to make
more precise and to complete the expression *in persona Christi*. It is in this quality that the priest presides over the Christian assembly and celebrates the
Eucharistic sacrifice "in which the whole Church offers and is herself wholly offered."[53]

The priest "first represents Christ himself." This is
the crux of the matter. Here the defenders of the traditional
male priesthood have elaborated their case with great detail
and incisive precision. The celebrating priest becomes the
very image of Christ.[54] Though it is ultimately the Lord who
acts, he acts by the tongue and the hand of the priest. Hence
the priest is the indispensable, irrefutable *sign* of the
exalted, invisible Lord. And that is why ordination is called

[53]*The Order of Priesthood*, pp. 14–15.
[54]In the Greek Orthodox literature the priest is viewed as the "icon"
of Christ, from the Greek εἰκών, meaning "image."

a sacrament and the priesthood regarded as sacramental in nature. As "Inter Insigniores" affirms,

> The Christian priesthood is therefore of a sacramental nature: the priest is a sign, the supernatural effectiveness of which comes from the ordination received, but a sign that must be perceptible and that the faithful must be able to recognize with ease. The whole sacramental economy is, in fact, based on natural signs, on symbols imprinted on the human psychology: "Sacramental signs," says Saint Thomas, "represent what they signify by natural resemblance." The same natural resemblance is required for persons as for things: when Christ's role in the Eucharist is to be expressed sacramentally, there would not be this "natural resemblance" which must exist between Christ and his minister if the role of Christ were not taken by a man: in such a case it would be difficult to see in the minister the image of Christ. For Christ himself was and remains a man.
>
> Christ is of course the firstborn of all humanity, of women as well as men: the unity he reestablished after sin is such that there are no more distinctions between Jew and Greek, slave and free, male and female, but all are one in Christ Jesus (see Gal. 3:28). Nevertheless, the Incarnation of the Word took place according to the male sex: this is indeed a question of fact, and this fact, while not implying an alleged natural superiority of man over woman, cannot be disassociated from the economy of salvation: it is, indeed, in harmony with the entirety of God's plan as God himself has revealed it, and of which the mystery of the Covenant is the nucleus.[55]

"Inter Insigniores" and its expositors make frequent appeal to the tradition of the church (understanding tradition as much more than mere custom and venerated usage)

---

[55]*The Order of Priesthood*, p. 12. When the Declaration was first published, the point that there must be a "natural resemblance" between Christ and his ministers was lampooned by cartoonist Conrad—himself a Catholic—in a *Los Angeles Times* cartoon showing Pope Paul holding a baby Jesus drawn in his own image (see the *Los Angeles Times*, February 1, 1979, Part II, p. 5).

in support of their conclusion that women cannot be priests. But they readily admit that tradition is not enough. Hence they put the major emphasis on the thought, stated above, that the priest is the visible sign of the invisible Christ. With this thought, Roman Catholic theologians are confident to have gone beyond the *that* of tradition to the *why* of tradition. Yet, even so, they acknowledge that the conclusions to which they come are not a matter of "demonstrative argument" but of "profound fittingness." If the priest, when he pronounces the words of consecration in the Mass, is the very image of Christ Jesus, then it is only fitting that he should be a man and not a woman, for Jesus was a man and not a woman. Granted that humanity is essential to the Incarnation, the sexual character of that humanity cannot be ignored; it too is essential inasmuch as sexual distinctions are profoundly imprinted on the created order. In the fullness of time the Son of God took on our flesh, from whose pierced side, as it were, the church was born, even as Eve was born from Adam's side. And this church is his bride and he the Bridegroom who loves her and gives himself for her. Thus, in the pervasive symbolism of Scripture, the mystery of Christ and the church is indissolubly bound up with the unfathomable mystery of our being as male and female:

> That is why we can never ignore the fact that Christ is a man. And therefore, unless one is to disregard the importance of this symbolism for the economy of Revelation, it must be admitted that, in actions that demand the character of ordination and in which Christ himself, the author of the Covenant, the Bridegroom and Head of the Church, is represented, exercising his ministry of salvation—which is in the highest degree the case of the Eucharist—his role (this is the original sense of the word *persona*) must be taken by a man. This does not stem from any personal superiority of the latter in the order of values, but only from a difference of fact on the level of functions and service.[56]

---

[56]*The Order of Priesthood*, pp. 13–14.

The church, then, has no authority to institute a change in the order of ministry of the sort required for the ordination of women to the priesthood. The sacraments are to the church what natural law is to the secular realm.[57] While many women who seek access to the ministerial priesthood are no doubt motivated by a commendable desire to serve Christ and the church, they should not suppose that the priesthood is a matter of individual rights, as the Enlightenment has taught moderns to believe. The priestly office cannot be changed by human, social progress, for it belongs to another order of reality. And that order is revealed finally in Jesus Christ, who, being himself a man, chose men and only men to be his apostles. The church must be faithful to the example of her Lord. She cannot, therefore, consider herself authorized to admit women to priestly ordination.

> This practice of the Church therefore has a normative character; in the fact of conferring priestly ordination only on men, it is a question of the unbroken tradition throughout the history of the Church, universal in the East and in the West, and alert to repress abuses immediately. This norm, based on Christ's example, has been and is still observed because it is considered to conform to God's plan for his Church.[58]

"Inter Insigniores" concludes with a call to all Christians to meditate on the real equality of the baptized, an equality which in no way implies identity but rather recognizes that in the differentiated body of the church, there are distinct roles to be exercised in love. Observing that the greatest in the kingdom are not the ministers but the saints, the authors of the Declaration close with this word to Christian women:

> The Church desires that Christian women should become fully aware of the greatness of their mission:

[57]"The Church has no power over the substance of the sacraments, that is to say, over what Christ the Lord, as the sources of Revelation bear witness, determined should be maintained in the sacramental sign" (Pope Pius XII, as quoted in "Inter Insigniores," *The Order of Priesthood*, p. 9).

[58]"Inter Insigniores," *The Order of Priesthood*, pp. 10–11.

today their role is of capital importance, both for the renewal and humanization of society and for the rediscovery by believers of the true face of the Church.[59]

3. An Appraisal of the Argument

As we turn to an appraisal of the argument just summarized, we would commend those who framed it for their clarity and sobriety. Though it is an argument upholding the tradition, its tone is not demeaning or patronizing. Women are not viewed as creatures in whom there is some spiritual deficiency, creatures only modestly endowed with the powers of rational discretion. While appreciative of this fact, some have expressed disappointment that the Declaration contains nothing new. But this is not necessarily a fault. Serious students of theology know only too well the pitfalls of contemporary faddism in theology. To us the problem is not with the traditional form of the argument but rather with its intrinsic nature, particularly as it moves from sign to thing signified, a problem which is not infrequent in theological disquisitions of this sort.

As it is developed in the Declaration, the argument purportedly rests (as we have noted) not on a rigorous rational demonstration but on the revelation of God's will, both in nature and in grace, and the fitness of those signs and symbols in the natural order which give sacramental expression to that revelation. And, as we have further noted, so far as the ministerial priesthood is concerned, these symbols arise out of our human existence as male and female; a woman, to be specific, cannot be a fitting sacramental sign of Jesus, since Jesus was a man. But this argument from symbolic fitness and propriety cannot be made to yield results so certain as to be beyond question. Being Protestant, we can only venture—but venture we do—that were we Roman Catholic, we would find the argument in "Inter Insigniores" plausible, but by no means final and conclusive. We must now give ourselves to the task of stating why this is so—

[59]*Ibid.*, pp. 17–18.

why, specifically, it appears to us that even with a Roman
Catholic view of priestly ordination, there is no decisive
theological reason to exclude women from the ministerial
office. In short, we shall try to make good our earlier conten-
tion that women should have access to the office of ministry
whether that office be understood in Protestant or in Roman
Catholic terms.

The argument in "Inter Insigniores" is a specific instance of the general approach which infers a male order of
ministry from the masculinity of God. In our evaluation of
that argument, we observed that while theologians have said
that God transcends all sexual distinctions, it has proven
difficult for them to apply this insight consistently. If God is
likened to a human mother, the analogical nature of such
language is readily perceived; but when he is likened to a
father, the analogy somehow is different. God may be *like* a
mother, but God *is* a Father. By the same token, when the
church is likened to a bride, the analogical nature of such
language is readily perceived—insofar, that is, as we are talking about *men* in the congregation of God's people. But
when we are talking about *women*, again the analogy somehow is different. They are not the bride of Christ in the same
analogical way as are men because women *are* brides.

This is the root problem, as we see it, with the argument of the Vatican Declaration on women and the priestly
order; it is an argument which is constantly moving back
and forth from the symbolical to the literal and from the
literal to the symbolical in an *ad hoc* manner. There is no
critical control of the reasoning process at this point. The
argument is predestined to come out to a certain end because those who use it tack both from left to right and right
to left as they face the winds of counter-argument. Citing,
for example, the biblical data which speak of the relationship of God to his people in nuptial figures—Christ is the
Bridegroom who loves his bride the church—the text of the
Declaration says, "That is why we can never ignore the *fact*
that Christ is a man."[60] Here we move from symbol to fact

---

[60]"Inter Insigniores," *The Order of Priesthood*, p. 13 (italics ours).

in a simplistic, non-critical way. Symbols, of course, are related to facts, but a statement like this simply presupposes that the relationship is self-evident. Since Christ may be likened to a bridegroom (symbol), he became (in the Incarnation) a man (fact). And since, in fact, he became a man, he may be likened to a bridegroom (symbol).

Not only in the Vatican Declaration, but also and especially in the larger literature defending the Declaration, one finds appeal to certain self-evident facts as though these facts had the self-evident meaning the church has traditionally given them. How often one reads: it is a fact that Mary was not chosen to be an apostle; it is a fact that all the apostles were men; and so on. Now no one can dispute these facts as *facts*; the problem has to do with the interpretation of the facts as symbols. A fact, in the context of this discussion, is something which is *literally* so; a symbol is something which is *analogically* so; and this difference should give the careful thinker pause as he moves from the one to the other.[61] Take for example, the following:

> The New Testament, in spite of the chance of total renewal which it provides for women as well as for men, never testifies that a woman could be, in a public and authorized way, representative of Christ. To no woman does Jesus say, "He who hears you hears me." To no woman does he make the promise to ratify in heaven what she has bound or loosed on earth. To no woman does he entrust the ministry of public preaching. To no woman does he give the command to baptize or to preside at the communion of his Body and Blood. To no woman does he commit his flock.[62]

[61]By a "fact" we understand a tangible reality viewed in a way that suggests nothing beyond itself. By a "symbol" we understand a tangible reality which suggests an intangible reality beyond itself, the analogy between the two being the basis of the suggestion. Hence our statement, "a symbol is analogically so"; that is, a symbol is a symbol because of its analogy to the reality it symbolizes.

[62]Jean-Jacques von Allmen (a French Calvinist) as quoted by Kallistos Ware (a Greek Orthodox) in the latter's essay, "Man, Woman, and the Priesthood of Christ," in *Man, Woman, and Priesthood*, p. 71. We note the disparity of ecclesiastical tradition as illustrative of the thesis that the

Here one is confronted with a series of facts—Jesus never said this and he never did that—facts whose meaning (supposedly) is self-evident. These facts constitute irrefutable testimony (supposedly) that Christ, as Head of the church, never has and never will grant to any woman the right to speak in a public and authorized way as his representative.

But now suppose we were to say,

> To no *Gentile* does Jesus say, "He who hears you hears me." To no *Gentile* does he make the promise to ratify in heaven what he has bound or loosed on earth. To no *Gentile* does he entrust the ministry of public preaching. To no *Gentile* does he give the command to baptize or to preside at the communion of his Body and Blood. To no *Gentile* does he commit his flock.

Are these not facts also? Is it not so that Jesus never said any of these things to a Gentile? Of course it is so. But, we are assured, this is a fact which has only historical significance. But how can we be sure this fact has only historical significance? Is such a conclusion self-evident? What if one were to suggest that perhaps the exclusively Jewish character of the apostolate is to be understood, as its exclusively male character has been understood, as having a profound theological and symbolical significance? Surely there is evidence in the Scriptures that this is the case. God, in the new creation of grace, redeems the old creation of nature by making a unique and lasting covenant with Abraham, the progenitor of the Jewish race, and with his seed. Hence Jesus, as the Seed of Abraham *par excellence* (Gal. 3:16), had to be a Jew. And by the same token, his apostles had to be Jews. Is not this evident from the fact that he chose them to replicate, as it were, his own self, so that they not only spoke in his name (Mark 6:6b–13), but those who received them received him (Matt. 10:40)?

And one can further argue the theological fitness of an

---

issue of women in ministry is not, in the last analysis, a matter of Protestant vs. Catholic views of the ministerial office.

exclusively Jewish apostolate in that the number of the apostles was exactly twelve, constituting them as the new patriarchate, the seminal form and foundation of the new Israel of God to which Paul makes reference in Galatians (Gal. 6:16). This is evident not only in the promise that in the day of final restoration they shall sit on twelve thrones judging the twelve tribes of Israel (Matt. 19:28), but also and especially in the choice of one to take the place of Judas in filling out the original apostolic college with exactly twelve members. Could a *Gentile* have been chosen to take Judas' place? Would there have been a "fitness" in such a choice? Could a *Gentile* have symbolized the truth that the church is the new Israel of God, built upon the foundation of the apostles and prophets (Eph. 2:20) and therefore to be likened to a city whose walls have twelve foundations bearing the names of the twelve apostles of the Lamb (Rev. 21:14)?[63]

To this question, "Could a Gentile have been chosen to be one of the twelve apostles?" the answer must be, "Yes, of course." For all the theological "fitness" and "symbolic significance" attaching to the original apostolate as the foundation of the new Israel, i.e., the church, Judas' successor could have been a Gentile, had there been one who qualified in other respects for the office. And we know this not only because the present "successor" of St. Peter is a Gentile, but because, as a matter of fact (to stay with facts), there is testimony in other parts of the New Testament (the Acts and the Epistles) that Gentiles, such as Titus, were entrusted with the duties of the ministerial office. But what is the significance of this added fact? To this question the answer is given that this added fact proves that we cannot take the prior fact—Jesus entrusted the apostolate to Jews only—as having anything but historical significance. The

---

[63]Here see the articles, "Apôtre" by Xavier Léon-Dufour and "Israël" by Pierre Grelot in *Vocabulaire Theologie Biblique* (Paris: Les Editions du Cerf, 1962), a work representing, in our opinion, some of the best Roman Catholic biblical theology. We cite this source not only because of its scholarly competence but also because we desire to respond to "Inter Insigniores" in terms of Roman Catholic rather than distinctively Protestant thought.

fact that Jesus and all the original disciples, to whom he entrusted the authority to preach, absolve, baptize, and celebrate the Eucharist, were Jews, is theologically inconsequential so far as Gentiles are concerned. The exclusively Jewish character of the apostolate is a matter of time and circumstance, not an inviolable truth of revelation. Therefore Gentiles, as well as Jews, are properly ordained as successors of the apostles. Indeed, had Jesus been in the circumstances Paul found himself in, in his Gentile mission, he would have done as Paul did when he entrusted the ministry in Crete to Titus, an uncircumcised Gentile (cf. Titus 1:5ff.; Gal. 2:3).[64]

And why can we be sure of this interpretation of the facts? Because Gentiles are spiritual Jews and fleshly circumcision is nothing in Christ. Does not the apostle Paul say as much? "He is not a Jew who is one outwardly, neither is that circumcision which is outward in the flesh. But he is a Jew who is one inwardly and circumcision is that of the heart, in the spirit and not in the letter, whose praise is not of men but of God" (Rom. 2:28–29). In this passage in Romans he simply spells out the implications of his earlier affirmation that in Christ Jesus there is neither Jew nor Greek, for all are one in him (Gal. 3:28). In other words, not the physical fact of circumcision but the spiritual reality of a new heart and life in Christ is what qualifies a man (whether Jew or Greek) to serve in the ministerial office as a successor of the apostles. We are talking, of course, of real flesh and blood men who visibly symbolize and therefore constitute a "sign" of dominical authority in the church as the ordained successors of the original apostles. But that visible, tangible symbolism is not ethnic and fleshly in the sense that the "sign" could not be recognized for what it signifies were these men not circumcised in the flesh as were Jesus and the original apostles.

But if spiritual circumcision is what is essential to

[64]Not only was Titus uncircumcised, but the apostle refused to circumcise him to mollify the Judaizers. Thus his Gentile status became a test case. Cf. Gal. 3:15–20.

qualify men for ministry, why are women excluded when they meet the same qualification? Indeed, how is it that we can so easily recognize Jesus, a Palestinian Jew of the first century, in black Zulu or yellow Chinese priests, so long as they are males, but not in a female, even thought she were Jewish and her ancestors had lived in Palestine since the first century? The reason must be that the difference between male and female is of another order of significance from that of Jew and Greek. This is indeed the case, according to the official teaching of the Roman Catholic Church. Hence the Vatican Declaration, commenting on the saying of Jesus that in the resurrection they neither marry nor are given in marriage (Matt. 22:30), reminds the reader that this does not mean

> that the distinction between man and woman, insofar as it determines the identity proper to the person, is suppressed in the glorified state: what holds for us holds also for Christ. It is indeed evident that in human beings the difference of sex exercises an important influence, much deeper than, for example, ethnic differences; the latter do not affect the human person as intimately as the difference of sex, which is directly ordained both for the communion of persons and for the generation of human beings. In biblical Revelation, this difference is the effect of God's will from the beginning: "male and female he created them" (Gen. 1:27).[65]

In other words, God did not create humankind Zulu and Chinese as he created them male and female. Here it should be noted that those Protestant theologians who advocate the ordination of women would agree. Sexual distinctions are, indeed, more profound than ethnic ones. When God created humankind in his image and likeness, it was as male and female (Gen. 1:27), not as Jew and Greek. But the question before us is not the profound significance of the Creator's act whereby we are given our humanity in a fel-

[65]"Inter Insigniores," *The Order of Priesthood*, p. 14.

lowship of male and female, but rather, "How does this fact bear on the priestly office of ministry? Why is it that the so-called particularity of the Incarnation, whereby the Christ was born a specific human being, allows us to ignore his Jewishness but not his maleness?" The answer to this question is of crucial importance. And it is at this crucial point that the argument is not rigorously controlled, but rather (as noted above) moves between the literal and the symbolical in an uncritical manner. Let us see how this is so. Following the example of Louis Bouyer, Hans Urs von Balthasar, a member of the "blue-ribbon panel of Church leaders and theologians" who, in a collection of essays, elaborate and defend the decision of "Inter Insigniores," argues as follows:

> While man, as a sexual being, only represents what he is not and transmits what he does not actually possess, and therefore is, as described, at the same time more and less than himself, woman rests on herself, she is fully what she is, that is, the whole reality of a created being that faces God as a partner, receives his seed and spirit, preserves them, brings them to maturity and educates them. One can question this thesis of Bouyer in many ways, and we will do so elsewhere. But in the first place its central point is certainly to be accepted, all the more so in that it represents the core of an ecclesiastical tradition, which is free here of all peripheric scoriae and obscurities resulting from Hellenistic misogyny (which is partly re-echoed in the Fathers of the Church and in the Middle Ages). . . .
>
> Here, too, the principle holds good that "gratia supponit naturam." Restored nature would bring to light—within the parity of nature and parity of value of the sexes—above all, the fundamental difference, according to which woman does not represent, but is, while man has to represent and, therefore, is more and less than what he is. Insofar as he is more, he is woman's "head" and, on the Christian plane, intermediary of divine goods; but insofar as he is less, he depends on woman as a haven of refuge and exemplary fulfillment.

It is not possible here, for lack of space, to show in detail this difference in equality of nature; in particular, one would have to discuss the question of the masculinity of Christ, in his Eucharist, in which he, on a plane above the sexes, gives himself to the Church entirely as the dedicated seed of God—and the participation, difficult to formulate, of the apostolic office in this male fertility that is above sex. Only if this aspect were fully brought to light, would man's latent inferiority to woman be overcome in some way. But it must suffice here to mention this concept.[66]

Here the (supposed) fundamental difference between the man and the woman is, at last, spelled out according to the classic Roman Catholic understanding of the "Eternal Feminine."[67] And this difference is that the man (as male) "only represents what he is not and transmits what he does not actually possess." By contrast, the woman (as female) "is fully what she is, that is, the whole reality of a created being. . . ." Now if one grants that the created order should be understood *sub specie aeternitatis* (which we do), then, indeed, our humanity finds its ultimate meaning in openness to the Divine, self-surrender in humility to God our Maker. But—and this is an important "but," in our way of thinking—why should the woman *literally* exemplify this truth, as the above analysis suggests, and the man *symbolically*? How, in other words, does one get from fact to symbol in such an instance so that we can say the woman does not represent but *is* what she is (the creature), resting fully on herself; whereas the man *represents* what he is not (the Creator), and therefore he and he alone can be entrusted with the priesthood?

If the answer be given that in the mystery of redemption it was the Virgin Mother who by her *fiat mihi* (be it unto me) *cooperated with* the Divine while her Son *oper-*

---

[66]"The Uninterrupted Tradition of the Church," *The Order of Priesthood*, pp. 81–82.

[67]For an elaboration and critique of this concept, see the Epilogue to the author's *Man as Male and Female*.

ated as Divine, then, we must further ask, "How is it that von Balthasar can say that this masculine Christ (the Son) is 'on a plane *above* the sexes' and that the apostolic office participates 'in this male fertility that is *above* sex'?" If the whole matter is *above* sex on the divine side, then why is sex so significant on the human side? Furthermore, is not the argument skewed by the fact that the man's sexuality is understood symbolically (this *masculine* Christ, this *male* fertility, somehow transcends sex—is "above sex"), whereas the woman's sexuality is understood literally? Why is it that no woman can ever get above her sex? Why is it that femininity can never function "on a plane above the sexes"? And how is it that von Balthasar can affirm a "parity of nature and parity of value of the sexes," yet at the same time insist that the man, and the man only, is the "intermediary of divine goods" and therefore the "head" of the woman? Arguments like this one reflect the sort of *sic et non* one frequently encounters in the literature defending an exclusively male priesthood.

The reasoning of Gustave Martelet, S.J., member with von Balthasar of the above-mentioned panel of theological experts, exemplifies the same problem. Martelet argues,

> When the Prophets reproach Israel with her infidelity in terms of prostitution—remember the famous 23rd chapter of Ezekiel—they are speaking *literally*, for in the Covenant, God actually became the Bridegroom of his chosen People. (The text of the Congregation for the Doctrine of the Faith recalled this so clearly that I can be content with an allusion here.) The Covenant is, therefore, a mystery of such deep union between the Lord God and the members of his People that the conjugal life of man and woman is still only an image of the tradition, extraordinary in itself, which defined the Lord as a fiancé, a Bridegroom, and Israel as a fiancée and a *real* Bride, though unworthy.[68]

---

[68]"The Mystery of the Covenant and Its Connections with the Nature of the Ministerial Priesthood," *The Order of Priesthood*, p. 105 (italics ours).

But how can this be? How can the prophets be speaking *literally* when they call God a Bridegroom and accuse Israel as his unworthy bride? If Israel (and the church) is *literally* a wife, a *"real* bride," then would not the lay*men* in the church really be *women*?

As we have already observed, Israel cannot possibly be literally both the "wife" and the "son" of Jahweh.[69] Hence we understand such ways of speaking as figurative. But, as we can see from the above quotation, it would appear that for Roman Catholic theologians, the one figure is more "literally" true than the other. Israel is not a "son" in the same mysterious way she is a "wife." Likewise, if we follow Martelet's reasoning, Christians who constitute the church are not "all *sons* of God through faith in Christ Jesus" (Gal. 3:26) as they are betrothed to Christ as a chaste *virgin*, a pure *bride* to one husband (II Cor. 11:2). While it would seem obvious that the apostle is speaking symbolically in both instances, there is evidently a difference between the two. Even though both figures are sexual, the church is not male (son) in the same way she is female (virgin). But when we take such language more literally in some instances (the church *is* female, Christ *is* male) and less literally in others (Israel is *like* a son to God, God is *like* a mother to Israel), we encounter all kinds of nonsense. If, when speaking of Christ and the church as Groom and bride, we inject weighty theological significance into the literal fact that Christ was a male of the human species, then, when we change the figure and speak of Christ and the church as Head and body, we have the anomaly of a male Head and a female body. If it is replied, "Of course the church is not *literally* a female," then why press the point that Christ is *literally* a male? As a matter of fact, every once in a while even the experts, who so plausibly state the case for a male priesthood, seem to waver on this matter. They do not press the maleness of Christ, but pass over it as of little account. This, to us, appears highly significant and quite damaging to the argument for an exclusively male priesthood.

[69]See above, p. 38.

Joseph L. Bernardin, still another member of our panel of experts (also the Archbishop of Cincinnati and President of the U.S. Episcopal Conference), makes a very discerning comment in this regard. Noting that the Declaration views the priest as a sacramental sign that must be easily recognized by the faithful because of a "natural resemblance" between the thing and the thing signified, he goes on to say,

> The "natural resemblance" between Christ and his ministerial priests must not stop merely with the fact that they share a common masculinity. The ministerial priest acts not *"in masculinitate Christi"* but *"in persona Christi."* If he is to be an effective sign, especially if he is to lead and inspire others, particularly women, in the apostolate, then he must display the virtues and the godlike qualities of the man Christ. It is not maleness that must be accented and brought forward as the significance of the priesthood, but rather Christlike qualities; humility, gentleness, self-effacing service must be easily recognizable.[70]

This is, indeed, an insightful observation. The Archbishop insists that the natural resemblance between Christ and his priests must not stop merely with the fact that they share a common masculinity. Our question is, "Why must it *begin* there?" If the faithful cannot see Christ in a male who exemplifies no godlike virtues—humility, gentleness, and self-effacing service—can they not see him in a female who does? Indeed, if the priest acts *"in persona Christi,"* not *"in masculinitate Christi,"* then *"natural* resemblance" between Christ and the priest, it would seem, does not entail

---

[70]"The Ministerial Priesthood and the Advancement of Women," *The Order of Priesthood*, p. 117. Similar in thrust is the statement of Kallistos Ware that when we speak of a priest as an icon (image) of Christ, we must remember that "an icon is not the same as a photograph or a realistic portrait; and so, when the priest is considered as an icon, this is not to be understood grossly in a literal or naturalistic sense. The priest is not an actor on the stage, 'made up' to look like Christ" ("Man, Woman, and the Priesthood of Christ," *Man, Woman, and Priesthood*, p. 80). But is not the element of literalness always present in the argument, and that in a rather gross way, when so much is made of the maleness of the priest because Jesus was a male?

physical, that is *sexual* resemblance, but a resemblance which is natural to the *spiritual* order with which the worshiping congregation has to do. And in this order there is neither male nor female, even as there is neither Jew nor Greek. We would, therefore, conclude that since the Word was made flesh, as the apostle John has declared (John 1:14), we rightly heed those who, in the flesh, symbolize his presence as they speak and act in his name. But we see no reason to add to what the apostle said by insisting that the Word was made *male* flesh, for both male and female are equally bearers of the divine image. And since God created humankind in his image, male *and* female, we can only conclude that women as well as men should be ordained to the priesthood, because femaleness, like maleness, is a fitting symbol (sacramental sign) of Deity.

V.
The Woman's Right to the Order of Ministry Affirmed

A. INTRODUCTION

History, including church history—one might almost say *especially* church history—has always had its great women, whose lives have witnessed to the woman's potential as an achiever. But it has been relatively easy in the past to ignore these beacon signs by putting such women in the special category of the exceptional and charismatic.[1] Gradually, however, as science and technology have lightened the burdens of motherhood, it has become increasingly apparent that women who are neither geniuses nor charismatic are capable of many things simply because they are human beings in the image of God, with all that that implies for their powers of self-transcendence and their God-given right to a responsible expression of it.

It was John Stewart Mill, in his essay on "The Subjection of Women," who first questioned the assumption that

[1]Not all past female achievement has been on the part of a few gifted individuals. E. Franklin Frazer, the great authority on black American history, once observed: "After Emancipation, when the whole social fabric of life crumbled and the very economic basis of Negro existence was destroyed, it was the Negro woman ... who made the survival of the Negro possible." As quoted by Mrs. Medgar Evers, "Profiles of Negro Womanhood," *Negro Heritage Library* (1964), 1:12. This black, female achievement, of course, has made little impression on the lordly, white male.

the woman's failure to produce anything of the highest rank
in philosophy, science, or art, was due to her natural incapability. Men greeted his doubts with a cool smile.[2] But a
hundred years later, it is not Mill's doubts that seem preposterous but the arrogance of his peers who contemned them.[3]

Not that the evidence is all in, but it has become
increasingly clear that it is her general situation in society
that explains the woman's lesser accomplishments. She is
born into a man's world and must compete on his terms.
And because her future so much depends on the good plea-
sure of the man, it is tempting for the woman to gain value
in his eyes by tightening the reins on the impulse of her own
achievement as a person. Even when she takes the initiative,
even when she does excel, she must *appear* not to do so,
since the insecure male is threatened by the blue-stocking,
the brainy, intelligent, superior woman. It is no easy matter
for the woman to manage this conflict between her social
role and her essential humanity. To enter into life moved
with hope and ambition, while appearing passive, dependent, and submissive, makes her a walking contradiction.
Little wonder that more women do not attain the highest
plateaus of which they are capable. Beginning by feigning
immanence, to use Simone de Beauvoir's term, in the end
they lose their transcendence. They become the victims of
Betty Friedan's "problem that has no name."

And when the woman becomes aware of her problem,
when she is able to give it a name, the solution to her problem is anything but simple. How can the woman, who is
aware of the unjust limitations imposed upon her sex, submit to them without impairing her humanity, her inalien-
able right to do all that she is capable of doing as a human
being? But if her determination to overcome these limitations hardens into defiance, her effort will become counter-

[2]See "The Subjection of Women," in *Essays on Sex Equality,* ed.
A. S. Rossi (Chicago: University of Chicago Press, 1970), pp. 203ff.
[3]Alice S. Rossi, editor of Mill's *Essays,* complains that even down
to the present, scholars of Mill ignore the essay on women as "unessential"
to his thought (*ibid.,* p. 5).

productive; it will consume all her energy and thus impair her humanity even more.

Surely the church, as the company of God's people, should manifest its calling to be a redemptive force in the world by striving for full equality in the man/woman relationship. And, indeed, it has done so in that it embraces men and women alike in its fellowship, through faith in Christ, a faith confessed and confirmed in the rite of baptism, which knows no distinction of the sexes. But through the centuries the church has drawn back, being conformed to this world at one crucial point. We refer, of course, to the church's withholding from the woman the office of ministry with the authority and privilege which such an office implies.

The observation that the church, in this respect, has been "conformed to the world" is intended not so much as an indictment of the church's failure as a statement of the facts of its life. The church has intended to be a transforming and renewing power in the world in every respect, and indeed, in many respects it has been. But in this particular respect, it would seem, the church has construed the data of revelation through the eyes of the world more than through the eyes of faith. Because God has revealed himself in the figure of a father (though he also has revealed himself in the figure of a mother), and because he became incarnate as the man Jesus (though Jesus never related to women as the men who follow him have commonly related to them in the church), and because Jesus appointed men as his apostles (though as Head of the church he poured out his Spirit on sons and daughters alike that they should prophesy in his name), the church has assumed that God is so much more like the male than like the female that he can be adequately represented in the authoritative office of the ministry only by men. Thus the church has construed the data of revelation in a manner that has limited the woman's place in the family of God.

So long as this perspective prevails, the woman will never come into her full inheritance as a Christian. Her place will be that of assistant to the man rather than partner with him. Not that the work which she has rendered in this secondary role is unworthy of the Christian name or of little worth in God's sight; the self-effacing tasks of nurture and charity are supremely worthy in God's sight. But to limit women to the maternal role of teaching children and to the charitable service of the deaconate, when they know they have equal gifts and calling with men, is to threaten their Christian lives with banality.

And if men in the church cannot empathize with women in this problem, let them reflect upon what it has cost the church, of which they are the leaders, to use only the tithe of its female talent. Just to think that a Florence Nightingale, as a member of the church of England, should feel constrained to write to Dean Stanley:

> The Church of England has for men bishoprics, arch-bishoprics, and a little work (good men make a great deal for themselves). For women she has—what? I had no taste for theological novelties. I would have given her my head, my heart, my hand. She would not have them. She told me to go back and do crochet in my mother's drawing-room; or, if I were tired of that, to marry and look well at the head of my husband's table. You may go to the Sunday School, if you like it, she said. But she gave me no training even for that. She gave me neither work to do for her, nor education for it.[4]

Let anyone look in any hymnbook and see what women poets—Fanny Crosby, Charlotte Elliott, Frances Havergal, Christina Rossetti, Anna Steele—have taught the worshiping congregation to sing; and then ask what it would mean to the church if such women were allowed to move beyond the relative anonymity of the hymnal and achieve the visibility that men have had in the church as teachers, preachers, and evangelists.

[4]E. T. Cook, *Life of Florence Nightingale* (New York: The Macmillan Co., n.d.), 1:57.

B. WOMEN AND THEOLOGICAL EDUCATION

1. Introduction

What follows is really not theology but an effort to apply theology, an effort to make it relevant to the present need of the church. Whatever is relevant is not necessarily good theology, but good theology is always relevant and should never be done in detachment from the human situation. At the practical level, then, we must face the question, "How can the church overcome the sexism which has made the ministry the exclusive calling of the male?"

In another generation, the woman's right to vote was considered crucial to her winning a place in the sun. Today the economic factor is stressed: equal job opportunities with equal pay. But more basic than any other consideration is, perhaps, the woman's right to education of the same quality as is available to the man. It was an axiom of the slaveholder that slaves should never learn to read, and down to the present day black children receive inferior education to white children in the public sector. So it has been with women. Assuming that the man is the one "in whom the discretion of reason predominates," many concluded that the woman need not be educated at the same level as he. And since she was denied equal education with the man, it was easy to confirm the fundamental assumption that she lacked the critical abilities to receive such education.

Jean Jacques Rousseau declared, "The whole education of women should be relative to men. To please them, to be useful to them, to win their love and esteem, to bring them up when young, to tend them when grown, to advise and console them, and to make life sweet and pleasant to them; these are the duties of women at all times, and what they ought to learn from infancy."[5] As late as the 1920's, when the most liberal university in the American South, the

---

[5]Jean Jacques Rousseau, *Emile for Today*, chapter on "Marriage" (London: Wm. Heinemann Ltd., 1960), p. 135.

University of North Carolina, opened its doors to women, it was stipulated that they must: (a) be accompanied to class by a chaperone; (b) sit in a group in the rear of the room; (c) wear gloves and hats; (d) remain in their seats till the men had left; and (e) not participate in the graduation ceremonies nor have their picture in the yearbook.[6] The all-male student body overwhelmingly voted against their admission and the school paper editorialized that the school would be overrun with girls and succumb to "an effeminate influence of sentimentality."[7]

It is little wonder, in the light of such treatment, that many women have claimed to be satisfied in their dependent role. What else is to be expected when they are trained to think that their chief end is to be attractive to the man by showing a meek and submissive resignation to his will? And what is true of women in society is true of Christian women in the church. Denied access to quality theological education, they have not been able—and, in many instances, have not even desired—to share the responsibilities of the ministerial office with men. One place to begin, therefore, in overcoming the problem of sexism in the church is in the theological seminary.

2. A Historical Note

Turning to the matter of women's access to quality theological education, the historical record corresponds, understandably, to the theological stance of the church. Since it has been generally deemed improper that women should aspire to the calling of the ministry, they have been discour-

---

[6]In America, first in the West, then in the East, and finally in the South, women were admitted to institutions of higher learning.

[7]As for "effeminate sentimentality," Dorothy Sayers showed how sentimental woman can be when she responded to a question asked when Oxford debated concerning the admission of women to the student body. "Why," some men wondered condescendingly, "do women want to learn about Aristotle?" "*Women*," she replied, "do not want to learn about Aristotle—*I* want to learn about Aristotle." Sayers was a member of the first group of women to graduate from Oxford.

aged from pursuing the theological training open to men.[8] While those churches requiring little formal education for ordination have tended to be somewhat tolerant of women seeking access to the ministerial office, those that place a premium on an educated clergy have limited women, in their ministry, to benevolent societies devoted to social relief and foreign missions. As a result, many women, through the years, have sought ecclesiastical emancipation in nondenominational organizations such as the Young Women's Christian Association and the Women's Christian Temperance Union. In 1887 Frances E. Willard, president of the WCTU, wrote:

> When will blind eyes be opened to see the immeasurable losses that the church sustains by not claiming for her altars these loyal, earnest-hearted daughters, who, rather than stand in an equivocal relation to her polity, are going into other lines of work or taking their commission from the evangelistic department of the Women's Christian Temperance Union?[9]

At the time, such pleas were largely ignored; and even though the situation has since improved, so far as formal admission to theological studies is concerned, only a beginning has been made in the admission of women to the ranks

---

[8]As early as 1675, Robert Barclay argued that anyone whose mouth is opened by the Spirit has the right to exhort, reprove, and instruct the assembled congregation "whether rich or poor, servant or master, young or old, *yea, male or female.*" "Seeing male and female are one in Christ Jesus, ... when God moves by his Spirit in a woman, we judge it no ways unlawful for her to preach in the assemblies of God's people." See his *Apology for a True Christian Divinity,* the exposition of Proposition X, sec. XXIV, XXVII. This enlightened sentiment is found in a broadside where Barclay is repudiating "the carnal ministry of men's making," whereby a certain class of men called clergy "are educated and brought up as other carnal artists" to monopolize things and the rest are despised as laymen. Naturally, therefore, since he was deemed a heretic for such radical views of the ministry in general, his feminist sentiments confirmed rather than convicted the church in its traditional opposition to the ordination of women.

[9]As quoted by Dorothy Bass Fraser, "Women with a Past: A New Look at the History of Theological Education," *Theological Education,* vol. 3, no. 4 (Summer, 1972), p. 216.

of the ordained clergy. There are many reasons why this is so, ranging all the way from the formal problems of altering canon law to the pragmatic prejudices, so often heard, that women preachers cannot sustain the nervous strain, do not have voices that can be heard, hamper their husbands' vocational freedom, create conflicts in marriage, impede the progress of church union, and the like.[10]

One obvious reason why the church has made such minuscule progress in "claiming for her altars her loyal, earnest-hearted daughters" is the character of the theological seminary and the way in which it has conceived its task. For all its limitations, the seminary is really the only institution where one can ordinarily obtain the theological training which academically qualifies one (there are many other qualifications, of course) to hold the office of ministry and exercise the responsibilities of leadership in the church. But the seminary has been for males by intent and purpose. And this intent has traditionally been conceived as reflecting a *divine* intent. But if our logic is sound, if (a) women have every right to share the leadership of the church with men, and if (b) they can never achieve such a place of leadership apart from full access to the privileges and prerogatives of the ministerial office, and if (c) their access to this office depends, among other things, on their receiving the same academic training that men receive, then obviously the seminary will remain a bottleneck until its self-image is altered so that women have full citizenship in this elite academy of theological scholarship. This transformation of the seminary, already begun in terms of liberalized admis-

[10]To classify such matters as "prejudices" is not to deny that they have some correspondence to fact. The prejudicial character of such arguments consists in their application to women *as a class*. If they were applied individually, then such arguments would fail, since *some* men, like *some* women, cannot sustain the nervous strain of the ministry, cannot be heard (in which case they use a microphone), hamper their wives' vocational freedom, create conflicts in marriage, and impede the progress of church union. In fact, the arguments between *men* from differing ecclesiastical traditions over the validity of their respective views of ordination have sometimes not only *impeded* church union, but brought it to a screeching halt.

sion policies, will come only gradually at a deeper level because male prejudices are, in some respects, so primordial that they become indistinguishable from those theological convictions that all Christians rightly cherish and seek to preserve.[11] These prejudices are not insurmountable, but they can be overcome only as women are given the opportunity to prove themselves in places of leadership in the church, an opportunity which these very prejudices tend to deny them by withholding education from them. Hardly an ideal situation!

In this regard, the story of Antoinette Brown, the first woman to be ordained in America, should be required reading for all male seminarians. Brown attended Oberlin Collegiate Institute, which was noted for its "liberalism" as the first co-educational, privately controlled, denominational school in the United States. Convinced from her study of the Bible that women could enter the ministry, and having finished her college work, she sent tremors of consternation through her alma mater by applying for admission to the seminary:

[11]For many years Fuller Seminary, where the writer teaches, refused the regular divinity degree (B.D.) to women. The catalogue stated, "The Bachelor of Sacred Theology degree (S.T.B.) is offered for women upon completion of the standard theological curriculum with the exception of certain courses (such as Pastoral Theology), for which substitutes are made. The conferring of this degree must be preceded by the attainment of a standard bachelor's degree on the college level."

Thus women had to compete with men when they entered the institution while being deprived of equal status with them when they finished their course of study. This arrangement, understandably, did not attract many women. Then one day an astute male student (a Danforth scholar) who wished to be excused from taking practical courses in order that he might enrich his academic electives came into the writer's office. He argued that the catalogue did not expressly exclude men from the S.T.B. program. His exposition of the text of the catalogue being unimpeachable, he was consequently granted permission to skip the ministry courses after the example of the women. Immediately, a modest line formed behind him. As a result, from 1965–1968 all candidates awarded the women's S.T.B. were men! This trend so disconcerted the ministries division that the degree was terminated in 1969; and women, the incidental beneficiaries of these all-male maneuverings, began, for the first time, to homilize in the sacred halls of Fuller Seminary.

Meeting after meeting was held to devise ways of keeping her out but the charter stated that all privileges open to men were also open to women. (The assumption had been that women would not want anything but a short literary course. But semi nary!) Finally, Professor Morgan of the Department of Biblical Literature was delegated to tell her that they would have kept her out if they could, but since that was impossible, they would do their very best to teach her.[12] The Ladies' Board, composed mostly of professors' wives, did not give up so easily. A rule was made restricting graduate students from teaching undergraduates in an effort to limit means of self-support for women. Antoinette's parents disapprovingly withdrew their assistance. She was refused a license to preach. Other help came, however, and she graduated in 1850; but the seminary would not list her name with the men. Years later, however, she was listed with her class; in 1878 she was awarded an honorary Master's degree, and in 1908 was made a Doctor of Divinity.[13]

When Brown, having graduated from seminary, tried to speak at the World Temperance Convention in New York

---

[12]Though such treatment was surely unconscionable, it was advanced for its time. If one finds this hard to believe, let one consider the editorial comment in the *New York Herald* evoked by the convening of the Woman's Rights Convention in Syracuse, New York, Sept. 12, 1852, two years after Oberlin graduated Brown. The *Herald* described the Convention as "the farce enacted at Syracuse." The newspaper went on (a) to affirm that the woman is subject to the man "by her nature and her sex, just as the Negro is and always will be, to the end of time, inferior to the white race, and, therefore, doomed to subjection . . . "; (b) to ask what the leaders of the Convention wanted; (c) to answer its own question by observing that they wanted to fill the posts which men are ambitious to occupy. The editor concluded: "How funny it would sound in the newspapers, that Lucy Stone, pleading a case, took suddenly ill in the pains of parturition, and perhaps gave birth to a fine bouncing boy in Court! Or that the Rev. Antoinette Brown was arrested in the middle of her sermon in the pulpit for the same cause, and presented a 'pledge' to her husband and the congregation . . ." (see *The Borzoi College Reader*, ed. Charles Muscatine, 3rd ed. [New York: Alfred A. Knopf, Inc., 1976], pp. 332f.).

[13]Elsie Gibson, *When the Minister Is a Woman* (New York: Holt, Rinehart & Winston, 1970), p. 18.

City (1853) as a delegate, Horace Greeley, a reporter who was present, satirized the result in the following words:

> This convention had completed three of its four busi-
> ness sessions, and the results may be summed up as
> follows: First Day—Crowding a woman off the plat-
> form. Second Day—Gagging her. Third Day—Voting
> that she shall stay gagged. Having thus disposed of the
> main question we presume the incidentals will be
> finished this morning.[14]

Impressed with Brown's ability, Greeley and Dana, editors of the *New York Tribune* and the *New York Sun*, offered to provide her with a hall in New York City and a salary of $1,000 a year if she would preach there regularly. She declined, considering herself too inexperienced, and went to South Butler, New York, where she served the local Congregational Church for three hundred dollars a year. In the same year (1853) she was ordained. Two years later she married and eventually became the mother of six children. Though marriage terminated her official ministerial functions, her husband, a prosperous merchant, encouraged her to continue her professional work. While rearing her children, she wrote ten books and took part in various reform movements.

3. Women Seminarians, Catalysts of New Structures in the Church

Antoinette Brown's history is not so remote from the present as one might suppose. Elsie Gibson reported in 1970 that among ordained women responding to her questionnaire, the oldest ones said they had faced situations only a little less acute than the one Brown faced.[15]

---

[14] *Ibid.*, p. 19.

[15] *Ibid.* Gibson reports, p. 24, that Elsie Johns, a Methodist pastor in Michigan, when asked by her bishop to see if she could revive a dying church, found a building with every window broken and no heating plant. On the pulpit a note had been left: "There are no members and no money. Here's the key." After door-to-door calling and facing an empty church for

A first step, of course, in changing this situation is the recruiting of women for theological education. Virtually all Protestant seminaries have taken this step (at least women are tolerated in seminary, if not recruited). But such a step, important as it is, does not alter the fact that the theological seminary has traditionally been so "white, male, and clergy-dominated"[16] that it will be so, more or less, for a long time to come. Seminaries are much more given to the preservation of tradition (which is by no means all bad) than to innovation and change. Change, in contrast to tokenism, will come only gradually, as a larger female presence among seminarians results in a correspondingly significant female presence at the teaching and administrative levels. This larger female presence in the enterprise of theological education will, in turn, increase the challenge to—perhaps one should say pressure upon—the institutional church to open to competent and trained women the same opportunities afforded to competent and trained men. In this way the *quo vadis* which women who pursue higher theological education face will be resolved.

Unfortunately, but inevitably, this resolution will be achieved only through suffering on the part of those who have already suffered so much, for the path from the ivory halls of theological academia to positions of leadership in the church will be strewn with special obstacles for the woman. She will have to cope with (a) the prejudices of lay people as well as those of her peers, which will be difficult if she is sensitive; (b) limited professional possibilities and low remuneration, which will be difficult if she is talented and self-supported; and (c) the great paucity of single Christian men who are secure in the light of her education and vocational desires, which will be difficult if she desires mar-

---

four Sundays, she was finally greeted by two mothers bringing their children to Sunday school. Twenty-five years later (1970) she was serving the same church with well over a thousand active members.

[16]The description is Marvin J. Taylor's, as a result of his study of seminaries in the AATS in 1970–71. See his comments, "Theological Education," *AATS Quarterly*, VIII (Autumn, 1971), 1.

riage.[17] Yet the woman who lacks these qualities—sensitivity, talent, discipline—can hardly become a leader anywhere, especially in the Christian church.

Those women, therefore, who desire to share the office of Christian ministry with men must be prepared to pay the high price that will be exacted of them. To say less would be naive. But to say more would be to despair, and Christians should never despair. They "ought always to pray and not to faint" (Luke 18:1). Some women, however, have despaired and not only shaken the ecclesiastical dust off their liberated feet but also renounced the faith by which to guide their feet. It is to be hoped that the majority will not do so, for Christian men will never be relieved of their prejudices save as Christian women compel them to be by continuing to press for their privileges as children of God. And in this struggle they must be able to meet men on their own turf. They must be not only committed to the Christian faith, as godly women have always been, but trained and able to interpret their faith. They must be able to spell out its implications and make it relevant in their situation with a critical insight that will not be contemned and cannot be gainsaid.

Thus, and only thus, will Christian women enter into their full inheritance as children of God; and as they do so, Christian men, the traditional custodians of authority in the family of God, will relinquish their prejudices and share their privileges in the church. Thus the church will become in deed, as in theory, a fellowship which knows no male and female, worthy of the name *communio sanctorum*. Of course, Christian men, being the offenders, have no claim upon their sisters in Christ that they should minister to them through such redemptive suffering. The necessity laid upon the women who have served and will serve the church in this way must come from their Lord, the Head of the Church, who summons them to the task with "gifts and calling that are without repentance" (Rom. 11:29). And when such women shall so serve the church, then Frances Havergal will be seen

[17]And should she meet such a rare man and marry him, she will be criticized as unfaithful to her calling as a wife if she continues in the ministry.

to have spoken better than she knew when, in 1887, she wrote the beautiful words,

> Take my voice and let me sing,
> Always, only, for my King.
> Take my lips, and let them be
> Filled with messages from Thee.

ADDENDUM: A THEOLOGICAL COMMENT ON MOTHERHOOD

We began our discussion by observing that through the centuries of church history, the Fathers and theologians of the church disqualified the woman from the office of Christian ministry by virtue of her very nature as female. We have found some of their reasoning to be not only unconvincing but also unworthy of the gospel, the good news that in Christ there is no male and female. This good news, however, does not mean that the difference between the sexes is done away in Christ. The new humanity, reconciled by his Spirit, is male/female humanity still. Hence men and women fellowship as men and women in Christ's church. Though the old antagonism is removed, the difference between them remains, both as a biological fact and as a calling in life. The Christian faith, in other words, redeems the difference between the sexes, seeking to make it the basis of mutual enrichment; it neither fears nor despises it.

One result of this sexual difference is the more rigorous demand which the preservation of the species makes upon the woman. At puberty a young woman undergoes a biological transformation that not only endows her in most cases with less sheer muscular strength than the average man has, but also initiates a rhythm in her life that may be accompanied by pain and fatigue.[18] When she is pregnant, she carries within herself another self until the moment of

---

[18]Much has been said (by males) about the psychic instability induced by female menstruation. Of course, men, too, have varied temperaments, not wholly unrelated to some complex physiological chemistry beginning at puberty. The majority of males, it has been said, fluctuate not once a month with the moon, but every day with the sun!

hold

birth, which is a moment of labor and struggle for many, and for some a moment of even greater sacrifice. And birth marks the beginning of the demanding task of motherhood. As mother, the woman nurses the newborn infant at her breast and bends much of her initiative, aggressiveness, and inventiveness to serve and nurture her offspring. Obviously, then, it is not as easy for the woman to transcend the act of procreation as it is for the man. This fact has significant implications for her as a member of the human species. While it in no way lessens the woman's humanity, it does mean that she faces a unique challenge as she seeks to express that transcendence, spontaneity, and creativeness— that freedom under God to "have dominion over the fish of the sea . . . and over every creeping thing . . . upon the earth" (Gen. 1:26) which is of the essence of life as fully human.

In other words, because the woman is the mother, *as a class* women do not have the same amount of freedom men have to pursue other tasks in life. But the grand fallacy is to infer from the differing biological roles which men and women have in the ongoing enterprise of life that the woman has a fixed, inevitable destiny wherein she is dependent on the man and, "knowing her place," must seek to fulfill herself in obedient submission to him, while the man, being independent of the woman, is free to understand himself apart from her and free to understand her in terms of himself.[19] *Motherhood, as a biological fact, no more determines the meaning of woman's existence than fatherhood determines the meaning of man's existence. The meaning of all human*

[19]We would suggest that this tendency to define the woman in terms of her biology rather than her humanity is what has provoked much of the so-called feminist reaction to virginity and motherhood, a reaction typically deplored by Cardinal Joseph Ratzinger in his defense of the Vatican decision against women priests: "It is significant that the two qualifications in which the particular way and dignity of femininity are expressed in an unchangeable way—virginity and motherhood—should be slandered and ridiculed in an unprecedented way today. In other words: the two fundamental ways of being in which woman, in a way granted to her alone, expresses the high point of being human, have become forbidden concepts, and anyone who brings them positively into action is suspected *a priori* of obscurantism" ("The Male Priesthood and Women's Rights," *The Order of Priesthood*, p. 135).

existence, that of the man and the woman alike, is freedom under God in the fellowship which the very form of our humanity as male and female implies. In other words, we hold the difference between maternity and paternity to be a penultimate rather than an ultimate fact of our humanity as male and female. However, since it is a fact, and one having a significant bearing on the woman's call to ministry, it seems appropriate that we should comment further on motherhood as it bears specifically on the woman's call to ministry.

"And Adam called his wife's name Eve," we read in Genesis 3:20, "because she was the *mother* of all living." There can be no doubt that in the Old Testament the ideal of womanhood is not simply to be a virgin, or a wife, or a mother, as though the woman were free to choose for herself. These three ideals of womanhood are not of equal worth; rather, they build on one another. While the first (virgin) and the second (wife) are both praiseworthy, a woman's fulfillment, *qua* woman, is as a mother.[20] It would be easy to dismiss this strand of revelation as simply the by-product of patriarchal culture, which assigns the woman the one and only task which the man cannot perform and exalts her to a special honor for performing it in order to compensate her for being deprived of self-fulfillment in the many other ways open to the man. On the other hand, it would also be easy to absolutize this strand of revelation by insisting that the woman is so uniquely fulfilled in motherhood that if she does not achieve this state, she comes short of the Creator's revealed purpose for her life when he made her a woman. We wish to sketch a theology of motherhood between these two extremes.[21]

[20]Here it should be noted that the queen *mothers* in the Old Testament were always named. From bits of information preserved in the historical narratives, it would seem that as a class these women were the most influential in Israel, often wielding great power behind the throne for good or evil.

[21]The best statement we have read on the theological meaning of motherhood in Israel is Katherine von Kirschbaum's *Die wirkliche Frau* (Zurich: Evangelisher Verlag, 1949), ch. 4. Some of our thoughts are drawn from this source.

First of all, we suggest that the high evaluation of motherhood in the Old Testament has as its mysterious and underlying *raison d'être* the fact that God's covenant promise of salvation could achieve its fulfillment only in and through the holy generations of Israel, culminating in the birth of the Messiah, the seed of Abraham *par excellence.* [22] The unique role of the woman in all this is hinted at in the reference to the woman's seed in the *protevangelium* (Gen. 3:15) and in the prophetic oracle concerning the young woman with child (Isa. 7:14). It is strikingly confirmed in the birth of our Lord, a birth achieved not without God's help, but quite without a man's help. And the word to Joseph in Auden's poem, "For the Time Being," is a rebuke to all male arrogance:

> For likening Love to war, for all
> The pay-off lines of limericks in which
> The weak resentful bar-fly shows his sting,
> For talking of their spiritual
> Beauty to chorus-girls, for flattering
> The features of old gorgons who are rich,
> For the impudent grin and Irish charm
> That hides a cold will to do harm,
> Today the roles are altered; you must be
> The Weaker Sex whose passion is passivity.
> . . . .
> You must learn now that masculinity,
> To Nature, is a non-essential luxury. [23]

But now that the promise has been fulfilled in that the Virgin has brought forth the Son whose name is Immanuel, God with us (Matt. 1:23), motherhood, like fatherhood, has no longer the significance that it had in the Old Testament. Parenthood in the New Testament recedes into

---

[22]Of course, if this is true, then the covenant promise implies an equally high evaluation of fatherhood in the Old Testament. And such is the case. Male prejudice appears, not in the premium put on begetting and bearing children in the Old Testament, but in the assumption (in ancient Israel) that the woman was *made* for bearing children and that the man did the woman a favor in begetting children of her.

[23]*Collected Longer Poems* (London: Faber & Faber, 1968), p. 152.

the background, having fulfilled its primary purpose in holy history. Hence the genealogies of Jesus are the last to be written. Hence, also, celibacy is a Christian option, and a childless marriage is a true marriage. One's chief end is "to glorify God and to enjoy him forever," whether one is married or not married, a parent or not a parent. *And this is just as true for the woman as it is for the man.* [24]

There is no way, therefore, from the perspective of Christian theology, to justify the manner in which the church has shut up the Christian woman to maternity as her only proper calling in life. If one does not believe that the church has done this, let him consider, among other things, the opposition traditionally registered by the church to birth control and the practice, even down to the present day, of giving single women who work for the church lower salaries and early retirements whenever the budget must be cut. What better way to encourage such women to seek husbands to whose children they can be mothers?

Not only should Christian women be free to be or not to be mothers, but when they choose motherhood, which many will continue to do, they have every right to use the help of advancing scientific knowledge to relieve the burdens which such a choice entails. This is just to say that they have the right to do what men have done who have relieved the burden of their toilsome labor with the help of science. In other words, while motherhood will always limit the woman in a way that fatherhood does not limit the man, this difference will not be as significant in the future as it has been in the past. Mothers with fewer children and a longer life expectancy will have a freedom to serve Christ and his church in much larger ways than in the past.

The church should grant such women responsibilities of leadership commensurate with their freedom, as God shall call and equip them to assume these responsibilities.

---

[24]We have italicized this sentence since everything else in this paragraph has been often affirmed. The last sentence, however, which is the most obvious, is *not* affirmed by many, who treat women as though *Mother's* Day were the holiest festival in the Christian year.

In doing so the church will not alter, but only extend, its theology of the ministerial office, for it has always recognized the compatibility of *paternity* with the exercise of this office.[25] It is in every way congruous, then, with such a theology, that the church should also recognize the compatibility of *maternity* with the exercise of this office.

What forms this enlarged responsibility of women will take can be learned only in and through the experience of giving them a share in the many tasks devolving upon those who enter the office of Christian ministry. Undoubtedly specialized ministries, as well as dual pastorates, some involving husband and wife, will increase in the future. As male hegemony over the office of ministry is relinquished, it must be remembered that the Christian woman who shares with the man the individualized form of the priesthood of all believers in Christ will do so *as a woman*. If the writer were to venture a prediction, it would be that men will have great difficulty at this point. Even those who are sincerely ready to share the ministry of the church with women will expect the woman in such a role to think, to speak, and to act *like a man*. But this is to misunderstand the meaning of sexual complementarity. Because God made humankind male and female, just as in the natural realm men are fathers and brothers and women are mothers and sisters, so it must be in the spiritual realm. As men who have been called and ordained to the ministry have been spiritual fathers in the church, so women will be spiritual mothers.

This difference will not affect the formal content of the Christian message, but rather the perspective from which it is seen and proclaimed.[26] The good news of the gospel and its proclamation are ultimately the same, whether the messenger is male or female. When the women on whom the Spirit came at Pentecost prophesied, their mes-

---

[25]When we make this latter affirmation, we are, of course, speaking as Protestants.

[26]This difference in the perspective from which the message is given will result, no doubt, in many details of the message that were hitherto overlooked and suppressed being brought into sharper relief.

sage was the same as the apostle Peter's.[27] And in more recent times, when women have composed hymns sung by the church universal, these hymns have had the same content as those composed by men. One may only guess, then, that a difference between men and women in the ministerial office may not be so much in evidence in preaching as in pastoral counseling. The application rather than the proclamation of the message will reflect more intensely the difference between spiritual fathers and spiritual mothers.[28]

Yet one can only speculate for want of evidence. The one thing that is certain is that as the office of ministry is

[27]In times past, to be sure, women have not shared with men in the profound formulation and elaboration of this message. They have rather been Sunday school teachers and, especially on the mission fields, teachers in Bible institutes and colleges. And Catholic Sisters have taught theology in parochial schools at the college level. (The *New Catholic Encyclopedia*, [New York, 1967], p. 939, observes that Theresa of Avila has popularly been given the title "Doctor," but not officially, since the teaching office in the church is limited to males.) But this will change, and there will be women counterparts to Barth and Rahner differing from them only in their Christian name Karl. This is simply to recognize what has already happened in science. Newton's *Principia* (1687) was popularized in a widely circulated book entitled *Newtonianism for Ladies*. Then came Mme. Curie, not just the first *woman* but the first *person* ever to receive the Nobel Prize in science twice (in 1903 with her husband in physics and in 1906, after her husband's death, in chemistry). In 1935 her daughter Irene Joliot-Curie received it jointly with her husband in the field of chemistry.

[28]In all of this the erotic factor will undoubtedly be present. Its mysterious power for good can only be surmised. In this regard it is instructive to read Sir Frederick Treve's description of the effect on John Merrick (the "Elephant Man") of his first encounter with a friendly woman. As he relinquished the woman's hand, Merrick "sunk his huge head on his knees and sobbed until Treves thought he would never stop: He told me afterwards that this was the first woman who had ever smiled at him, and the first woman, in the whole of his life, who had shaken hands with him. From this day the transformation of Merrick commenced and he began to change, little by little, from a hunted thing into a man."

This interesting account of how the touch of a woman, who was neither his nurse nor his lover, marked the turning point in Merrick's life "from a hunted thing into a man" is found in Ashley Montague, *The Elephant Man, A Study in Human Dignity* (quoted by Allesoin and Busby in *The London Times Literary Supplement*, June 9, 1972, p. 655). A similar moving story, also from real life, is *The Snow Goose* by Paul W. Gallico (New York: Alfred A. Knopf, Inc., 1941). However, in this latter instance, the man/woman relationship came to have something of the exclusive character of married love.

opened not only to those called to be fathers and shepherds to Christ's people, but also to those called to be mothers and shepherdesses, this will enrich rather than impoverish the life of the church. As in the natural family the ideal is to have both a father and a mother, so it is in the spiritual family which is the church. And ultimately this is so because the God who created humankind in his image as male and female is a God who both pities us as a father pities his children (Ps. 103:13) and remembers us as a mother who cannot forget her suckling child (Isa. 49:15).[29]

[29]Elsie Gibson's study, *When the Minister Is a Woman*, contains data gathered from about 270 ordained Protestant ministers who are women. The experience of these pioneers, working in twenty denominations ranging from Pentecostal to Unitarian—single, married, widowed, and in two instances divorced—indicates that women function as well as men in the ministry if they can overcome the parishioners' incredulity. Most church members interviewed, who had had women ministers, found them to be better listeners than men, less inclined to be self-assured, less impatient with modest results and less patronizing in their relationships with lay people. As administrators women pastors find it easier when they ask for help to get a positive response from the men. This is due, in some instances, to the latter's unconscious chauvinism. The limitations of sex are marginal and cancel out each other. Women cannot fraternize with men at the Kiwanis (a handicap?), but men cannot assist the bride in her preparations. A member of a small Methodist congregation in an Oklahoma town, unnerved by the intelligence that the bishop was sending a woman to be the new pastor, pondered the plight of the parishioners as she weeded her garden: "I had asked the good Lord to send us a fine preacher and he is sending a *woman*! Then I got to thinking—I had not specified male or female" (p. 87).

VI.
Epilogue: Theology and the Language of the Masculine

A. INTRODUCTION

In a remarkable manifesto Dorothy Sayers scathingly indicts the church for its demeaning view of women as "human-not-quite-human." The initial task, she avers,

> when undertaking the study of any phenomenon, is to observe its most obvious feature; and it is here that most students fail. It is here that most students of the "Woman Question" have failed, and the Church more lamentably than most, and with less excuse. That is why it is necessary, from time to time, to speak plainly, and perhaps even brutally, to the Church.
>
> The first thing that strikes the careless observer is that women are unlike men. They are "the opposite sex"—(though why "opposite" I do not know; what is the "neighboring sex"?). But the fundamental thing is that women are more like men than anything else in the world. They are human beings. *Vir* is male and *Femina* is female: but *Homo* is male and female.
>
> This is the equality claimed and the fact that is persistently evaded and denied. No matter what arguments are used, the discussion is vitiated from the start, because Man is always dealt with as both *Homo* and *Vir*, but Woman only as *Femina*.

I have seen it solemnly stated in a newspaper that the seats on the near side of a bus are always filled before those on the off side, because, "men find them more comfortable on account of the camber of the road, and women find they get a better view of the shop windows." As though the camber of the road did not affect male and female bodies equally. Men, you observe, are given a *Homo* reason; but Women, a *Femina* reason, because they are not fully human. . . .

Or take the sniggering dishonesty that accompanies every mention of trousers. The fact is that, for *Homo*, the garment is warm, convenient and decent. But in the West (though not in Mohammedan countries or in China) *Vir* has made the trouser his prerogative, and has invested it and the skirt with a sexual significance for physiological reasons which are a little too plain for gentility to admit. (Note: that the objection is always to the closed knicker or trouser; never to open drawers, which have a music-hall significance of a different kind.) It is this obscure male resentment against interference with function that complicates the simple *Homo* issue of whether warmth, safety, and freedom of movement are desirable qualities in a garment for any creature with two legs. Naturally, under the circumstances, the trouser is *also* taken up into the whole *Femina* business of attraction, since *Vir* demands that a woman shall be *Femina* all the time, whether she is engaged in *Homo* activities or not. . . .

Must we always treat women like Kipling's common soldier?

> It's vamp and slut and gold-digger, and
> "Polly, you're a liar!"
> But it's "Thank-you, Mary Atkins" when the
> guns begin to fire.

We will use women's work in wartime (though we will pay less for it, and take it away from them when the war is over). But it is an unnatural business, undertaken for no admissible feminine reason—such as to ape the men, to sublimate a sexual repression, to provide a hobby for leisure, or to make the worker more bedworthy—but simply because, without it all *Homo* (including *Vir*) will be in the soup. But to find satisfaction in doing good work and knowing that it is wanted is human nature; therefore it cannot be feminine nature, for women are not human. It is true that they die in bombardments, much like real human beings: but that we will forgive, since they clearly cannot enjoy it; and we can salve our consciences by rating their battered carcasses at less than a man's compensation.

Women are not human. They lie when they say they have human needs: warm and decent clothing; comfort in the bus; interests directed immediately to God and his universe, not intermediately through any child of man. They are far above man to inspire him, far beneath him to corrupt him; they have feminine minds and feminine natures, but their mind is not one with their nature like the minds of men; they have no human mind and no human nature. "Blessed be God," says the Jew, "that hath not made me a woman."

God, of course, may have his own opinion, but the Church is reluctant to endorse it.[1]

The church's reluctance to endorse God's opinion of women—a reluctance which it underlines by excluding them from the ministerial office—is a specific instance of the larger problem Sayers so astutely analyzes, namely, the reluctance of males to include females in the human race. God created humankind (*homo*) in his own image, male (*vir*) and female (*femina*) (Gen. 1:27). The man, however, tends to define all humanity in terms of himself, to the exclusion of the woman. And, as we have noted in our previous discussion, this tendency has led male theologians to assume that God himself is a masculine Deity, an assumption fortified by the very nature and structure of human language. Understanding

[1]Dorothy Sayers, "The Human-Not-Quite-Human," as quoted in *The Borzoi College Reader*, ed. Muscatine & Griffith, 3rd ed. (New York: Alfred A. Knopf, Inc., 1976), pp. 336–40.

himself as the primary paradigm of humanity, the male has learned to speak as though such were the case. This male-dominated language, as we have seen, has complicated the ongoing theological debate concerning women's ordination.

R. S. Turner, a woman sensitive to this problem, complains—and not without reason—that the words in our present vocabulary which unquestionably include the woman are those which make her sex her most notable attribute. Otherwise, that is, as a *human* being, she remains invisible. The words which stand for general, all-around identification, within whose meanings she is supposedly included ("man," "he," "him," "himself"), actually slip and slide from a general (human) to a specific (male) connotation. A term like "fellow man" can, upon occasion, be pulled out from under the woman's feet by being interpreted as "fellow males," thus reminding the woman of the fragile and intermittent nature of her inclusion in the human race.[2]

Having concluded that, for the present, the proper way to speak of God is to use pronoun "he" rather than "she" or "it," and having employed such usage throughout this discussion, we can only admit its inadequacy as we grant its seeming inevitability.[3] To grant its inevitablity for the present, however, is not to assume its finality for the future. As Christian women become more visible in the church—and they will when they are theologically trained and ordained to the office of Christian ministry—we may hope that the thought of the church about women , and even

[2]Cf. Rosa Shand Turner, "The Increasingly Visible Female and the Need for Generic Terms, " *The Christian Century*, March 16, 1977, p. 248. Turner is an instructor in English at the Episcopal Theological Seminary of the Southwest, doing graduate work in creative writing at the University of Texas. In this article she makes several helpful suggestions which, if followed, would relieve, if not resolve, the problem of sexist language.

[3]See above, the section on God and the Male Imagery of Scripture, pp. 35f. Lawyers, it seems, have not been unaware of the slippery character of the English personal pronoun in its masculine singular form. One such lawyer, C. C. Converse, in 1884, proposed the introduction of a new pronoun, "thon," formed by combining "that" and "one." Use of this form made sufficient headway to warrant its inclusion in *Webster's International Dictionary*, second edition, but it is not in the current third edition.

about God, will change. And with this change of thought, we may further hope, there will come a change of language also. Thus the church will have a more adequate medium for conveying the Christian message, a message which includes women with men as equals in the family of God and "heirs together of the grace of life" (I Pet. 3:7). In the meantime we can only deplore the insensitivity of those males who are impervious to the feminist plea that we not canonize traditional sexist language. Such insensitivity reflects the sad truth that those who inflict the wrong are seldom as aware of the fact as those who suffer it. A male of the species may protest that masculine language need not be heard in an exclusive way (and that, as a matter of fact, he does not so hear it), but how is he to know what it sounds like to the female of the species unless he listens to her when she tells him? And the time has come for men, who have always done the "talking" (while leaving the "prattle" to women), to learn to listen for a change. Men must learn to hear themselves as enlightened and sensitive women hear them in order that they may learn how to speak in a more truly Christian manner.

B. THE SHAPE OF THE PROBLEM

As we contemplate this needed change in linguistic usage, we should suffer no illusions about the difficulty of achieving it. Indeed, the problem is so complex that we venture the opinion that sexist language may never be wholly overcome by the church this side of the eschaton. Our reason for speaking thus is not far to seek. It has already surfaced in the preceding argument. In that argument we have noted the obvious fact that when theologians have spoken about God in masculine terms, they have emulated the example of the biblical writers. That is to say (and this is why the problem is so acute), theologians have spoken about God in the way he has (ordinarily) spoken about himself. This latter affirmation is the plain implication of the common confession of the church that the Bible is the word of God. Granted that he spoke in and by the words of a Moses, an Amos, an Isaiah;

yet it is *God* "who at sundry times and in divers manners
spoke in time past . . . by the prophets" (Heb. 1:1). Granted
that he spoke in and by the words of a Peter, a Paul, a John;
yet the early Christians heard the apostolic word "not as the
word of men, but as it is in truth, the word of *God*" (I Thess.
2:13). Yet we have concluded that the woman may—indeed,
should; indeed, must—be given equal privilege and responsibility in the church. "*She*" must be given the opportunity
to speak for this God to "*his*" people. And we have arrived at
this seemingly implausible, yet very definite, conclusion by
arguing that God so transcends all sexual distinction as to
be neither male nor female, yet appropriately *likened* to
both.

Our problem, as we see it, is not with the logic of
our conclusion, nor with its biblical character. Athens can
not fault it as a piece of invalid reasoning nor Jerusalem
accuse it as a denial of divine revelation. Were such criticisms
possible—that is, were the argument for the ordination of
women plagued by some hidden irrationalism or some
faulty hermeneutic—theologians would at least know how
they should proceed in attempting a possible resolution. But
the truth is, these traditional approaches will not help us
resolve the problem which the ordination of women presses
upon the church. And why not? Because it is a problem so
deep, subtle, and intractable as to be beyond the direct reach
of logic and the immediate scope of exegesis. It is the problem of language, not as an abstract exercise in semantics or
comparative philology, but as the indispensable medium of
communication, the very incarnation of thought. Specifically, we have in mind the primary, biblical language by
which God has revealed himself to us, and we, to whom the
revelation comes, have sought to speak his thoughts after
him. This language is heavily weighted on the masculine
side and has shaped our thought accordingly. And as
thought, in turn, shapes the human spirit, so Christian
thought shapes the Christian spirit because Christian
thought is nothing more or less than the material definition
of our faith, the "faith which was once for all delivered to
the saints" (Jude 3).

The relation of language to thought is, of course, no new problem. As for biblical language and biblical thought, critical, historical study of the Bible has shown how the biblical writers used language common to their culture and times to convey the uncommon truths of revelation, giving new meaning to old words. And even before Deissmann and others shed "light from the ancient East" on the language of Scripture, theologians knew that the truths of revelation are greater than the metaphors, analogies, and figures which the human authors of Scripture used to express such truths. The Holy Spirit, as Calvin says, lisps to us in Scripture, as a nurse to a child. But it is one thing to acknowledge this and to draw the quite valid conclusion that God, though revealed pre-eminently in masculine terms, is not a male Deity; it is another thing altogether to live out the implications of this conclusion. *God*, indeed, may transcend our male-oriented language; but *we* do not, or at least, we have not in the past. Had our fathers in the faith, both in the Old and the New Testaments, both in Israel and in the church, really succeeded in thinking of God as personal, but not as masculine; had they really succeeded in thinking of our humanity as given us in a partnership of male and female and not as a hierarchy of male over female; we would not so naturally speak of our *fathers* in the faith and so seldom of our *mothers*. But this is the way the church has always spoken, and this is the way we still speak. This is our inheritance, our language.

But, someone will say, it is self-evident that where there are fathers, there must be mothers; therefore, it is understood that when we speak of our fathers, we include our mothers in the term. When we speak of the God of Abraham, Isaac, and Jacob, we are speaking of the God of Sarah, Rebecca, and Rachel as well. Quite true. But this salvo does more to underscore our problem than to resolve it. Our linguistic usage, which names the fathers and leaves the mothers to a tacit assumption, reflects the more fundamental reality that Abraham, Isaac, and Jacob dominated patriarchal history (that is why it is *patriarchal* history) just as males have dominated all biblical history, including apostolic history and all post-apostolic Christian history down to the present time. *Heilsgeschichte* is holy history, but it is not altogether holy. It is a history in which God, indeed, has revealed himself as the Redeemer of his people, but at the same time it is a history which bears witness to the domination of the male over the female. And we are who we are, as the people of God, because our history is what it is. We cannot change that history and we cannot escape it; were we to do so we would no longer be the people of God.

But to say that we, the people of God, cannot change our past is not to say that we cannot change our future—or better, that God cannot change it. With him all things are possible. As he condescended to reveal himself in our past, fractured and broken as it has been by male arrogance, may he not redeem our future by leading the church into a more Christian practice of male/female partnership through the opening of the office of ministry to women whom he calls? And will not this increased visibility of women be reflected, in turn, in our language? Indeed, may it not be that a conscious effort to change our language may contribute to this more basic change of relationship in the Christian church?

Some will complain that to call on *God* to redeem our future is an evasion of our responsibility. *We* must learn, by doing, how to speak a new language, a more truly Christian language, which neither our fathers nor our mothers knew. The reason "he" has been used *generically* of God and "man" *generically* of the human family, is that the male, who is "he" and "man" *specifically*, has sinfully understood himself as the measure of all things. Therefore he has applied the masculine noun to the whole human race and the masculine pronoun to God himself. Assuming that God is a male, man has acted as though the male were God. Let us not, then, piously wait for heaven, "its wonders to perform"; rather, let us exorcise the demon of the ubiquitous masculine from our Christian vocabulary in order that the anonymous feminine may be delivered from bondage. Then, and only then, will women, mothers in Israel and the church, daughters not only of Abraham but also of Sarah—

and of God—attain visibility, have a name and a face worthy of their calling in Christ.

All this is well taken. But a word of caution would seem to be in order lest in our exorcising we cast out the devil by Beelzebub. We must never forget that the God who reveals himself in the Bible is not the Absolute of the philosophers, the Ground of Being. Rather, he is the God who speaks as personal Subject, saying *I* am who *I* am. Therefore, as we have argued above, the personal language used by the Christian church in speaking of God is indispensable. Given the limitations of this language, there has been no better word in the past, nor does there seem to be any better word in the present, to speak of this God than "he," understanding "he" as a generic personal pronoun.[4]

The argument that "he" is the best term available when referring to God will be pressed by some who are dismayed at the thought of purging our theological vocabulary of its pervasive masculinity. They will protest that the debate over sexist language is "much ado about nothing." The language of the church has served us well enough for nearly two thousand years and therefore will continue to

[4]Ruminating knowledgeably on the "bind" we are in when it comes to God-talk, Jean Caffey Lyles, a *Christian Century* editor, observes that the way one refers to God is a function of one's theology. Thus, while it is easy for some, it is difficult for others to refer to the Deity in ways that do not require third-person-singular pronouns. Many, for example, would have difficulty with the effort of James F. White (a worship specialist for the United Methodist Church) to eliminate pronouns entirely: "God gives Godself to us." She testifies that a sermon in which the preacher referred to God alternately as "he" and "she" had for her "the unpleasant side effect of calling up the disturbing image of God-Who-Suffers-from-Gender-Confusion." She admits to increasing doubts about the necessity, even propriety, of excising all masculine language about God from one's prose, and concludes, "The sight of a woman pastor breaking the bread or baptizing a baby may do more to shatter the idolatries of a male-dominated church than a year of liturgies with 'neutral' God-language." (See her "The God-Language Bind," *Christian Century*, April 16, 1980, pp. 430–31.) This last point about the redemptive possibilities of the female presence in the pulpit, at the Communion table and baptismal font is well taken. Better any day to hear a woman preach well on the parable of the prodigal son, the waiting father, and the unforgiving brother than to hear a sermon, like one endured by the writer, on the parable of the prodigal child, the waiting parent, and the unforgiving sibling.

serve us well enough in the future. While the weight of theological tradition has tacitly (if not overtly) construed masculine language about God literally, we need only to change our understanding of the words, not the words themselves. We can, indeed, we must, continue using traditional language in speaking about God, for it is the language God himself has taught us; however, we must not continue to think of the male as supremely the bearer of the image of God.

These two points of view—we must change our language; we need not and cannot change our language—are the two horns of our dilemma. To perceive our quandary in depth, one has only to remember that because the man has dominated the woman throughout the course of civilization, he has, as we have observed, dominated human language as well. And one does not easily divert the thrust of centuries of usage. This fact came home to the present writer some time ago when, as the speaker at a seminar on the women's movement, he was introduced by a woman whose understanding of the problem was exceeded only by the wit with which she relieved it. With disarming diffidence, protesting that she was not a linguist, she admitted to an irony that had dawned on her and which she had verified in her dictionary—the irony that she, a woman, should be leading a *seminar*. The word "seminar," she reminded us, is an off-shoot of the word "seminary" and, together with the word "seminal," comes from the Latin *semen*, meaning seed.

As I reflected upon that fact [she continued], I couldn't help wondering how it would be if these words had been related to female instead of male biology. Then they would have been based on the word *ovum* instead of the word *semen*. When one thinks of hatching ideas, that is not inappropriate. If our language reflected a feminine bias instead of a masculine one, I would have been leading an "ovumar" rather than a "seminar." Ministers would attend "ovumary" rather than "seminary." (Is it not just possible that a theological school is similar to an incubator as well as to a seed bed?) And we would hope for ovumal ideas rather than seminal ideas. In case all this strikes you as a bit hysterical, *that* is a word related to *female* biology. Like hysterectomy, hysteria refers to the womb. That was the organ assumed to be the source of the condition, you see. One reason I love both the English language and Charles Ives' music to the point of intoxication is their magnificent absurdity.[5]

"Magnificent absurdity" aptly describes our language, for it magnificently clothes our thoughts even as it unwittingly betrays some of our absurd prejudices. But there are no easy answers to the question of how to preserve the magnificence and purge the absurdities. As we have observed, while we may curb overt abuses, we cannot immediately change the endemic usage of centuries.

[5]Kathryn Lindskoog, speaking at the National Youth Workers' Convention, Los Angeles, October, 1976, sponsored by *Youth Specialties.* Lindskoog, a freelance writer and an authority on C. S. Lewis, has published numerous articles in Christian journals, some of them bearing on the question of sexist language.

We have from time to time alluded to the parallels between the treatment of blacks and women. The language problem is one more case in point. It is not just that black men are "boys" and all women are "girls." Even as men are given to "seminal thought" and women to "hysterical actions," so the good fairies that we meet in early childhood practice "white" magic and the bad ones, "black" magic. Bunyan's Flatterer is a *black* man whose *white* robe (in which he is disguised) falls off his *black* back when he leads Christian and Hopeful into his net (*Pilgrim's Progress,* ch. XVII). As the late Martin Luther King, Jr., once observed,

> Even semantics have conspired to make that which is black seem ugly and degrading. In Roget's Thesaurus there are some 120 synonyms for "blackness" and at least 60 of them are offensive— such words as "blot," "soot," "grime," "devil" and "foul." There are some 134 synonyms for "whiteness," and all are favorable, expressed in such words as "purity," "cleanliness," "chastity" and "innocence." A white lie is better than a black lie. The most degenerate member of a family is the "black sheep," not the "white sheep." Ossie Davis has suggested that maybe the English language should be "reconstructed" so that teachers will not be forced to teach the Negro child 60 ways to despise himself and thereby perpetuate his false sense of inferiority and the white child 134 ways to adore himself and thereby perpetuate his false sense of superiority (*Where Do We Go from Here?* [New York: Harper & Row, 1967], p. 41).

C. TOWARD A RESOLUTION OF THE PROBLEM

1. Introduction

A modest beginning to the resolution of the problem of sexist language in our Christian vocabulary can be made by editing out such language, wherever possible, in the two major books of the church, the Bible and the hymnal. The former is God's word to his people; the latter, their response to his word. This being the case, the task is obviously much simpler, theologically speaking, in the latter case, though the poetic form of hymns does not give one the freedom to edit at will without destroying the author's art. As for the Bible, the very fact that it is the word of God limits the church to the task of faithful translation at the verbal level. Yet even here there is room for improvement, as we shall seek to show.

2. Sexist Language and the Hymnal

As for the hymn book, surely we can stop singing,

> Rise up, O *men* of God!

and sing instead something like,

> Rise up, O *saints* of God![6]

Our hymns could be altered in many details with no loss of poetry and a little broadening of our theology. The third

---

[6]It is interesting to reflect how the author of this hymn, W. P. Merrill, makes the language of male and female work both ways simultaneously in the third stanza:

> Rise up, O *men* of God!
> The Church for you doth wait,
> *Her* strength unequal to *her* task;
> Rise up, and make *her* great!

When this hymn is sung in worship, *women* in the congregation, who are reckoned among the "*men* of God," are joined by the *men* in the congregation who, as members of the church, summon *her* to fulfill *her* task. Perhaps a woman can think of herself as among the *men* of God and a member of the Christian *brother*hood, as a man thinks of himself as belonging to the Church, the *bride* of Christ, who anticipates the parousia as *her* wedding day. Paul wrote to the Corinthian Christians, including the men: "I have espoused you as a chaste *virgin* to Christ" (II Cor. 11:2); and in stanza of Frederick W. Faber's familiar hymn, "Faith of Our Fathers," originally read:

> Faith of our fathers! Mary's prayers
>   Shall win our country back to thee;
> And through the truth that comes from God
>   England shall then, indeed, be free.

Inasmuch as Protestants have straightened these lines out so as to sing

> Faith of our fathers! God's great power
>   Shall win all nations back to thee;
> And through the truth that comes from God,
>   Mankind shall then, indeed, be free

we could edit them a little more and begin one or two stanzas

> Faith of our *mothers*! God's great power
>   Shall win all nations back to thee.

This would not only remind us that there have been women of exemplary faith in the church, but also relieve the monotony of using the phrase, "Faith of our fathers" eight times in four stanzas. Although we all enjoy singing fine hymns with which we are familiar in the form we have learned them, it is a fact that few hymns have come down to us without revision. While some of these revisions have been the hackwork of editors, inspired by theological provincialism, others have made for real improvement. Having accommodated these changes, including the fumbling touches, we should be willing to tolerate those poetic infelicities that will inevitably appear in the effort to relieve the traditional masculine accent in our hymnody. Surely some aesthetic loss can be endured in the service of theological gain.[7]

John's vision the saints in glory are described as *virgins* (Rev. 14:4). The limitations of language work both ways, it would appear. The difficulty is that such limitations most of the time have been made to work in favor of the male.

[7]It is one thing to tolerate aesthetic loss, another to advocate linguistic barbarities, as male chauvinists are wont to do, tongue-in-cheek.

Genuine difficulties can arise, however, when one attempts to solve all problems of sexist language in our hymns by simple fiat.[8] Just to declare, as some have done, that "generic usage of masculine nouns and pronouns is no longer acceptable," provokes the question: "Who found this out?" How, then, are we to sing the most familiar doxology? Should we sing

> Praise God from whom all blessings flow,
> Praise God all creatures here below,
> Praise God above ye heavenly hosts,
> Praise Parent, Child, and Holy Ghost?

Better not to sing it any more than to neutralize it as theology.[9]

The following example is, in our judgment, less than humorous: "We know that sexist language must go from *The Worshipbook*. I am willing to sing 'A mighty fort is our God, a cowwark never failing...'" (R. M. Archibald, "A Rose by Any Other Name...," *Monday Morning*, May 16, 1977, p. 6). *Monday Morning* is a magazine for Presbyterian ministers, published by authority of the General Assembly of the UPUSA Church, through its editorial offices, International Center, 475 Riverside Dr., New York.

[8]Speaking of difficulties, some, it would seem, are created not only by the efforts to eliminate sexist language, but also by the attempts to circumvent those very efforts. For instance, consider this curious classified ad appearing in a Hampshire, England, newspaper, placed by someone seeking a qualified woman without violating the Sex Discrimination Act, which took force December 29, 1975, in Britain: "Wanted, experienced storekeeper, either sex, provided that they have at least 5 years experience, are fluent in German and look like Marlene Dietrich in her early twenties." While such absurdities generally work, they sometimes miscarry. Eton College, the elite boys' school at Windsor, placed the following want ad in the "Slough and Windsor Express": "Somebody to help in the pantry and dining room: a *person* to share a flat with another woman." "All the early calls," the school matron complained, "were from men who obviously thought it was a jolly nice idea to be able to share a flat with a woman..." (see the *Los Angeles Times*, May 5, 1976, Part I-A, p. 7).

[9]For the suggestion that the masculine pronouns be eliminated by repeating "Praise God," three times, see *Women, Men and the Bible* by Virginia Mollenkott (Nashville: Abingdon Press, 1977), p. 69. While this is a possibility, it still leaves us with the critical last line, "Praise Father, Son and Holy Ghost," where the masculine language is strongest. To eliminate this line would deprive Christian congregations of their trinitarian confession and reduce their praise to the terms of a general theism. This is what we mean by neutralizing the doxology as theology.

EPILOGUE: THE LANGUAGE OF THE MASCULINE // **133**

Speaking of hymns and sexist language, hymn-writer Fred Kaan incurred the displeasure of certain Christian women as the author of a hymn approved by the World Council of Churches to be used in preparation for its Fifth Assembly. The Berlin Consultation on Sexism asked the Council (Recommendation 5) to eliminate the sexist language (the use of "his" referring to God and "man" referring to the human race) from the hymn. Kaan replied that such a procedure was akin to the censorship imposed on writers and artists living under totalitarian regimes who have their work arbitrarily judged by some ideological yardstick and declared unacceptable: "Those who are clamoring for a cleanup of language in this area are making themselves guilty of riding ideologically roughshod over artistic freedom."[10]

Mr. Kaan went on to observe that Recommendation 5, as phrased in English, would not translate well into other languages. Were he and his wife, for example, to worship in France on a Sunday, they would be addressed as *mes frères*, to be sure; but upon leaving church, should he be run down by a car, he would be *la victime*. Were he, on the other hand, to arrive home safely and report for military guard duty, he would be *une personne* functioning as *une sentinelle*—feminine words all. Should action be taken in such cases, he asked, by concerned males? The French, he replied, have too profound a respect for their language to tamper with it. For all the anomalies, they know what can and cannot be done.

Such an argument is really not relevant, it would seem, since the problem is not so much *grammatical* gender as *natural* gender, that is, gender which corresponds to sex. The lines in Kaan's hymn which the Berlin Congress on Sexism deplored did not involve *grammatical* gender, as did his illustrations from French, but rather *natural* gender.[11]

---

[10]"That Famous Recommendation 5," *Monday Morning,* December 2, 1974, p. 7.

[11]These lines read as follows:

When in his own image God created man

* * *

Man against his brother lifted hand and sword. . . .

However, Kaan's further protest that the offensive lines were taken directly from Genesis, so that in this respect his hymn was entirely scriptural, cannot be so easily dismissed. This observation focuses the question of sexist language at its most critical point for those who are Protestant and evangelical. This critical point is simply the character of biblical language and what to do with it, a question to which we must now address ourselves.

3. Sexist Language and the Bible

Language reflects reality, and behind the language of the Bible is the reality of that holy history in and through which God's redemptive purpose has been revealed. As we have already observed, it is a history by males and about males. Vast ranges of biblical narrative are taken up with accounts of men—what they thought, what they said, what they did. With a few exceptions (and we can no longer treat women as exceptions), women are satellites, ancillary stage props to the ongoing drama of *Heilsgeschichte*.[12] At the center of the stage are men—Adam, Noah, Abraham, Samuel, Moses, David, Elijah, Peter, Paul, John—and Jesus. Even when it comes to the propagation of the race, the one work where males have traditionally acknowledged the indispensable character of the female's help, the curtain calls are taken by men. Genealogical information in the Bible is information about fathers who beget sons. The wives and daughters, without whom there would be no fathers and sons, are seldom mentioned; and when they are, they are often unnamed.[13]

---

[12]The so-called "Writings" of the Old Testament reflect an androcentricity as pronounced as that of the historical narratives. As a result, the Old Testament exhibits a vast preponderance of masculine verb forms and pronouns. "It might be interesting," observes Mary Daly, "to speculate upon the probable length of a 'depatriarchalized Bible.' Perhaps there would be enough salvageable material to comprise an interesting pamphlet" (*Beyond God the Father* [Boston: Beacon Press, 1973], p. 206).

[13]The appendix of James Strong's *The Exhaustive Concordance of the Bible* (Nashville: Abingdon Press, 1973), lists approximately 9,750 instances of "he" and 1,025 of "she." "Him" and "his" occur approximately 13,850 times, "her" and "hers" approximately 1,550 times.

Although—given the position we have taken—this male orientation is not revelatory of the relative places of male and female in the ideal order of God's kingdom, it is a fact of history. As a result of such male orientation of the narratives, the names of God are masculine and take a masculine singular verb, and the vast majority of metaphoric references to God involve male images. God is a Father, Husband, Master, King, Shepherd. God's priests in the Old Testament are all male—and the sacrifices they offer to him are predominantly male sacrifices. Levitical law seems even to imply a hierarchy in that male lambs are required in the sin offering for a priest (Lev. 4:3), the people as a whole (4:14), and their rulers (4:23). By contrast, a female lamb may be used by an ordinary sinner (4:28, 32; 5:6). In the New Testament God's apostles are all males; and the first apostolic sermon (Peter at Pentecost) is addressed to "men" and "brethren" (Acts 2:14, 29), language that would be unacceptable in many church assemblies today.

To be sure, the direction in which redemptive revelation is moving can be seen in this momentous event (Pentecost) which marks the founding of the Christian church. Though Peter addressed his audience as "Men of Judea," he quoted a prophetic utterance which explicitly embraced daughters and maid-servants in the Spirit's effusion; and those who responded, "about 3,000 souls," were baptized, a rite to which believing women brought qualifications that they could hardly bring to the comparable Old Testament rite of circumcision. The momentous wrenching of the patriarchalism of the Old Testament has begun. But it is only a beginning. Even in heaven, according to the seer's vision in the Apocalypse, God's throne is immediately surrounded by four and twenty elders (πρεσβύτεροι)—males all—clothed in white, with crowns of gold upon their heads.

When one remembers that biblical language is the basis of all Christian language—devotional, liturgical, theological—and when one further remembers that this language simply reflects the biblical reality which is the basis of all Christian faith, one can appreciate something of the difficulties theologians face, as teachers of the church, whose task it is to frame answers to the question of sexist language and the Christian faith. But let us not despair. Rather, let us gird up our loins and see if, for all the difficulties, we can at least begin to answer the question: "What ought the church to do in the light of the facts of biblical language and the reality behind that language?"

We shall begin with a theological affirmation that underlies and thus controls the tentative suggestions we are about to make; that affirmation is that Scripture is God's word in human words.[14] This being so, we must acknowledge the human, cultural limitations reflected in the way in which God's word comes to us; yet, we must also acknowledge that the church stands under the word of God as it is given (that is, fixed in a written form) in the Holy Scripture. In other words, while the church has the task of translating Scripture into all languages wherein the gospel is preached, it does not have the freedom to alter the meaning of Scripture in the light of subsequent historical developments. It must rather bring all history, including its own history, under the judgment and scrutiny of Scripture. What are the implications of such a view for the translation of male-oriented language in Scripture? What follows is a *tentative* attempt to suggest an answer to this question by introducing a few familiar and, in some instances, difficult cases.

There are, to begin with, many texts which employ male-oriented language but need not be translated in the

[14]Those who do not hold to such a view of biblical inspiration and authority will, of course, have a different approach to the question before us. Likewise, ecclesiastical committees, made up of persons holding different theological points of view, will frame reports that reflect different theological pluralism. Witness, for example, the report, "Language About God, 'Opening the Door,'" made by the task force on sexist language of the UPUSA to the General Assembly of 1975. In the introduction one reads, "The report is not suggesting that we should change the language of the Bible. Rather, it suggests that we should be more accurate in our translation of the Bible...." We turn the page and read, "God is Spirit, and those who worship God (the Greek text says αὐτόν, "him") must worship in Spirit and truth" (John 4:24). "God" is the more accurate translation of αὐτόν? (See *Minutes of the General Assembly of the UPUSA*, Part I, New York, 1975, pp. 528ff.)

specifically masculine way that tradition has approved. In Romans 9:3–4, for example, Paul declares with moving pathos (in the words of the RSV),

> For I could wish that I myself were accursed and cut off from Christ for the sake of my *brethren* (ἀδελφῶν), my *kinsmen* (συγγενῶν) according to the flesh, who are Israelites, to whom belong the *sonship* (υἱοθεσία), the glory, the covenants, the giving of the law, the worship, and the promises; to them belong the *patriarchs* (πατέρες), and of their race, according to the flesh, is the Christ.

Here is a text which definitely reflects the male orientation of all of Scripture. But the translation unnecessarily aggravates this fact. Though it is a small matter (small matters can add up to large matters), there is no need to retain *kinsmen* when we have a perfectly good English equivalent, *kindred*.[15] As for *sonship*, while υἱοθεσία *may* be translated this way, there surely is no need to do so. The word literally means "adoption of sonship" and may be translated simply "adoption," as in the familiar King James rendering of this passage.[16]

But still the words "brethren" (ἀδελφοί) and "patriarchs" (πατέρες) are in the text, and we have argued that the church does not have authority over the text to alter its meaning in translation. Since we have argued in this way, does it follow that "brethren" must be translated "brethren" and "patriarchs," "patriarchs"? The answer would surely seem to be yes, if we are talking about meaning at the lexical level. But is this conclusion secure? Can we not argue that the meaning of this Scripture surely embraces sisters with brothers and mothers with fathers as those numbered

[15]That the Greek is in the feminine gender (ἡ συγγενής) is irrelevant, as can be seen from the fact that the Greek for *kinswoman* is ἡ συγγενίς (Luke 1:36). See above, p. 133, for our remarks on grammatical vs. natural gender.

[16]The RSV rendering of Romans 8:23, "adoption as *sons*," is equally unnecessary. The committee responsible for the text of the RSV will (we hope) alter such translations.

among the Israelites to whom belong the adoption, the glory, the covenants, the giving of the law, the worship, and the promises? Is this not really what we are saying when we insist that the masculine terms of Scripture should be understood generically, not specifically? Were the masculine terms here used construed in a specific sense, the meaning of the text would be palpably strained. In such a case, Paul intended to exclude women from Israel's benefits and to confess that he could wish himself accursed from Christ for the sake of his fellow male Israelites only, a view no one would seriously espouse.

But if it is necessary to say that in this passage, while the words "brothers" and "patriarchs" explicitly mean "brothers" and "patriarchs," yet they implicitly mean "sisters" and "matriarchs" as well, may we not translate the text so as to make what is implicit, explicit, without being accused of altering its meaning? Admittedly there are many pitfalls here, for what is implicit is not always clear in a given text. (Modern speech versions show how easily one can move beyond the objective task of the translator, which involves minimal interpretation, to become one who expounds the Scripture—as one subjectively understands it—while posing as a mere translator.) Perhaps in such instances translators could use some device like italics to show where they have added words, though not meaning, to the text. Then our passage would read as follows:

> For I could wish myself accursed and cut off from Christ for the sake of my brothers *and sisters*, my kindred according to the flesh, who are Israelites, to whom belong the adoption, the glory, the covenants, the giving of the law, the worship, and the promises; to them belong the patriarchs *and matriarchs*, and of their race, according to the flesh, is the Christ.

There are other texts, unlike the above, which are not so amenable to non-sexist translations. They are, theologically speaking, the difficult instances. An example is the Lord's Prayer, which begins with the familiar and comforting words, "Our *Father* who art in heaven" (Matt. 6:9). Undoubtedly the church needs to teach that God is as much like a mother as like a father, because the Scriptures warrant such teaching and it is long overdue. If this is so, then there can be no sound theological objection to addressing God in prayer not only as our Father but also as our Mother, since both terms are used analogically. (There would, of course, be vehement objection to such usage in most congregations at the present time.) In other words, in liturgical—and in private—usage we are free to pray according to the *intent* as well as the *ipsissima verba* of Scripture. That is why no one suggests that we should drop the doxology, "For thine is the kingdom, the power and the glory forever," from the Lord's Prayer, when we use it in worship, even though we now recognize that it is not a part of the original text of Scripture.

But our question is, "Does the church have the right to change the text of Scripture in translation from 'Father' (πατήρ) to 'Parent,' 'Guardian,' 'Helper,' or some other such word, in order to remove its masculine overtones? Our answer is a qualified no. And we make this answer not because we would opt for a wooden literalism, but because no other word conveys what the text means. We cannot validly argue that since we know that God stooped to reveal himself in and through the patriarchal culture in which the human authors of Scripture lived, and since we know how inadequate their (and our) perception of God has been, due to this patriarchal understanding, the only way to correct this misunderstanding is to substitute another word for "Father" when it occurs in the text of Scripture, even though that other word gives a different sense to the text.

Admittedly, given the inadequacy of the patriarchal view of God, some other word than "father" would be preferable to escape the implication that God is like a human father *rather than* a human mother. But to date, at least, we seem not to have such a better word. The compound Father/Mother is linguistically monstrous, in our opinion, and strains our conceptual powers. The word "Parent" (and even more so, words denoting other than a familial relationship) seem to us insipid, lacking the connotations of warmth and care. Further, "parent" means "father" *or* "mother," not "father" *and* "mother." On the other hand, the plural "Parents" offends the monotheism of the Christian confession, whereby God is always addressed in the singular. Hence we conclude that Matthew 6:9 should be translated, as it has always been, "Our Father who art in Heaven," though the church need not be bound in its liturgical and devotional usage by this translation of the text.

D. CONCLUSION

Of course such a conclusion will not satisfy the more radical feminist theologians. For them the traditional theological vocabulary of the church is beyond redemption. Rather than reinterpret such terms as "Father," "Son," "King," "Lord," "Master," when applied to God, they would simply replace them with non-sexist terms, not only in the liturgy of the worshiping congregation but also in the primary language of Scripture itself. As Mary Daly has complained, traditional language inhibits the woman's self-transcendence. She cannot submit to it without assenting to her own lobotomy.[17] Such feminist theologians have the same problem—in reverse—as C. S. Lewis, who, as an anti-feminist, felt *his* self-transcendence would be inhibited were he asked to think of God as "Our Mother, who art in heaven" and to see this thought embodied in a female priest leading the congregation in worship.

And so we conclude our epilogue, knowing full well we have not said the ultimate word. In theology—as the term itself implies—the ultimate word belongs to God in any case; the theologian can never speak more than a penultimate word. When it comes to the subject of this epilogue, theology and the language of the masculine, it may be that a male theologian cannot speak even a penultimate word. This privilege may belong to female theologians. And when

[17]See her "The Courage To See," *The Christian Century*, 88 (1971): 1110, and especially her *Beyond God the Father.*

we speak of female theologians, we have in mind not only those women who have joined and will join the elite circle of academicians who are members of theological faculties, but those who have stood and will stand in the pulpit to proclaim God's word to God's people. In the hope that their numbers may increase and to that end, we have written this essay on the ordination of women. Though the church in the past has repudiated its Florence Nightingales and treated its Dorothy Sayerses as not quite human, we sincerely hope that in the future it will give its daughters their full inheritance as the children of God. We can no longer simply smile condescendingly at the oft-quoted prayer of the little girl, "Dear God, are boys better than girls? I know you are one, but try to be fair."[18] Rather, we must assure Sylvia, who offered this prayer, that God is just as much like her as like a boy and that some day she may not only speak *to* God in prayer as a Christian, but also *for* him as a minister of the gospel, proclaiming to all who hear her that God is, indeed, a God who is fair.

[18]Eric Marshall and Stuart Hample, eds., *Children's Letters to God* (London: Collins, 1967), no page.

Index

Acts of Thomas, 48
Analogical use of language, about God, 40ff., 55f., 86, 95, 124f.
Apostles, all Jews, 59, 88f.; all males, 27, 32ff., 60; and the historical situation, 58f.
Auden, 114

Baillie, J., 56
von Balthasar, Hans Urs, 92f.
Barclay, R., 104 n.8
de Beauvoir, Simone, 12, 99
Bernardin, J. L., 96
Brown, A., 106f.

Calling to ministry, 14
Calvin, 19; on Mary, 32 n.8; on Isa. 49:15, 40; on Philip's daughters, 65; on language, 125
Chrysostom, 6
Church, bride of Christ, 83, 86
Curie, Marie, 117 n.27

Daly, M., 11f., 44; 134 n.12, 140
Danielou, J., 74 n.45
Deacons and deaconesses, 71ff.
Deity, masculine, 27f., 121; beyond sexuality, 124
Dorcas, 74

Eastern Orthodox, rejection of female ordination, 77f.
Elephant man, 117 n.28
Episcopal Church, on the ordination of women, 76f.
Eroticism, its redemptive potential, 117 n.28

Eternal feminine, 59 n.31, 92f.
Eucharist, Roman Catholic view, 79f.
Eve and Mary compared, 5

Fertility cults, 36f.
Friedan, B., 99

Gentiles, right to ministry, 59, 88f.
Gerlitz, P., 49
Gibson, E., 108 n.15, 118 n.29
Gnostics, Holy Spirit a female, 49f.
God, and masculine language, 35f., 44f., 135f.; and feminine language, 38f., 46; like father and mother, 41f.; masculine in nature, 44
Gospel According to the Hebrews, 48
Grammatical gender, in the Godhead, 43, 50 n.20; linguistically irrelevant, 133f., 151 n.16
Greeley, H., 108

Harkness, G., 59 n.31
Havergal, F., 110
Hierarchy (sexual) rejected, 2; assumed in antiquity, 5f.; used against female ordination, 14ff., 66f.; in Pauline thought, 66f.
Hippolytus, 49
Hodgson, L., 56 n.26
Holy Spirit, and gender, 45 n.17; as female, 47ff.; as a dove, 49f., 50 n.20; in Trinitarian speculation, 52f.; conceives Jesus, 52f.

143

Sex, its profound meaning, 29f., 90f.
Sexist language, 119ff., and the Bible, 123f.; problem of change, 128; specific suggestions, 134ff.; and the hymnal, 130ff.
Sexual complementarity, 116
Sweden, Lutheran Church of, 77 n.48
Symbols, their sacramental use, 85f., meaning defined, 87

Theological education and women, 102ff.
Theresa of Avila, 27, 117 n.27
Thomas Aquinas, 6, 17, 19f., 23
Thomas, W. D., 68f.
Titus, uncircumcised, 90
Tradition, and male priesthood, 82f.
Trible, P., 41 n.13
Trinity, and the *analogia relationes*, 26, 36f.
Turner, R. S., 122

Universal priesthood, 20f., 79f.; relation to priestly office, 80

Virgin birth, 114

Ward, B., 75
Ware, K., 77f., 87, 96 n.70
W.C.T.U., 104
Widows, 72f.
Willard, F. E., 104
Wisdom, hypostatized as feminine, 50f.; applied to Jesus, 51f.
Witches, 6
Woman's Rights Convention, 107 n.12
Women, and Jesus' resurrection, 61f.; and human transcendence, 99; and hymnody, 101, 117; as apostles and deacons, 70ff.; as prophets, 62f.; as theologians, 117 n.27; at Pentecost, 62f.; humanity of, 112f., 119f.; in the divine image, 46, 97; Old Testament role, 113f.; prospects in the ministry, 109f.; silent in church, 34; their unique contribution in ministry, 116f., 118 n.29; viewed as charismatic, 23, 63, 98; viewed as sex objects, 7ff.

Index of
Scripture References

Jeremiah
7:16ff. — 36
31:9 — 55
44:15ff. — 37

Ezekiel
13:17–23 — 63
23 — 94

Hosea
4:14f. — 36

Amos
2:7f. — 36

Malachi
1:6 — 38, 40, 55
2:10 — 38

Matthew
1:20 — 52
1:23 — 114
3:17 — 55
6:9 — 139, 140
7:24–27 — 51
10:40 — 88
19:28 — 89
22:30 — 91
23:27 — 41 n.14
23:34 — 51
28:9 — 61
28:10 — 61

Mark
1:11 — 55
6:6b–13 — 88
8:27–30 — 62 n.33

Luke
1:36 — 137 n.15
1:38 — 5
2:36 — 64
3:22 — 55
11:49 — 51
15 — 54 n.25
15:1–7 — 41, 54 n.25
15:8–10 — 41, 54 n.25
15:11–32 — 41, 54 n.25
18:1 — 110
23:49, 55 — 63
24:11 — 61

John
1:2–3 — 51
1:14 — 97
4:24 — 136 n.14
4:39 — 62 n.33
20:11ff. — 61
20:22 — 62 n.35
20:28 — 30
23:49, 55 — 63

Acts
1:4–5 — 62
1:8 — 59, 65
2:3–4 — 63
2:7 — 63
2:14, 29 — 135
2:17 — 63
2:17–18 — 23
2:22–34 — 61
2:32 — 62
6 — 71
6:1 — 73
9:1–6 — 62
9:39 — 74
9:39–41 — 73
10:41 — 61
11:30 — 71
16:14–15 — 70
19:6 — 64
21:8 — 71
21:9 — 64

Romans
1:16 — 59
2:28–29 — 90
5 — 5
5:5 — 58
8:23 — 137 n.16
9:3–4 — 137f.
11:29 — 110
12:6 — 64
16:1 — 74
16:1–2 — 70
16:2 — 74
16:3 — 70, 71
16:7 — 70

I Corinthians
1:24 — 52
1:30 — 52